D1534704

KIDS
FIGHT
CLIMATE
CHANGE

This is for you: the **#2minutesuperhero**

First US edition 2022

Library of Congress Catalog Card Number 2021946455
ISBN 978-1-5362-2348-4 (hardcover)
ISBN 978-1-5362-2349-1 (paperback)

21 22 23 24 25 26 LEO 10 9 8 7 6 5 4 3 2 1

Printed in Heshan, Guangdong, China

This book was typeset in Myriad Pro.
The illustrations were created digitally.

Candlewick Press
99 Dover Street
Somerville, Massachusetts 02144

www.candlewick.com

CANDLEWICK PRESS

KIDS FIGHT CLIMATE CHANGE

Act Now to Be a #2minuteSuperhero

MARTIN DOREY

ILLUSTRATED BY TIM WESSON

CONTENTS

INTRODUCTION: CALLING ALL FUTURE SUPERHEROES!............ 8

MISSION 1: COUNT YOUR CARBON.. 32

MISSION 2: YOU'VE GOT THE POWER....................................... 38

MISSION 3: FIGHT CLIMATE CHANGE AT HOME......................... 44

MISSION 4: FIGHT CLIMATE CHANGE WITH YOUR FOOD.......... 50

MISSION 5: FIGHT CLIMATE CHANGE WITH YOUR SINK, SHOWER, AND TOILET.. 58

MISSION 6: FIGHT CLIMATE CHANGE WITH YOUR (LACK OF) STUFF... 62

MISSION 7: FIGHT CLIMATE CHANGE WITH YOUR GADGETS..... 66

MISSION 8: FIGHT CLIMATE CHANGE WITH YOUR WARDROBE.. 68

MISSION 9: FIGHT CLIMATE CHANGE IN YOUR GARDEN............ 74

MISSION 10: FIGHT CLIMATE CHANGE WHEN YOU TRAVEL........ 82

MISSION 11: FIGHT CLIMATE CHANGE ON YOUR VACATION....... 90

MISSION 12: FIGHT CLIMATE CHANGE AT THE SUPERMARKET.. 94

MISSION 13: FIGHT CLIMATE CHANGE AT SCHOOL................... 98

MISSION 14: FIGHT CLIMATE CHANGE BY PLANTING TREES..... 104

MISSION 15: FIGHT CLIMATE CHANGE WITH YOUR MONEY....... 106

MISSION 16: FIGHT CLIMATE CHANGE WITH YOUR VOICE........ 108

BONUS MISSION: FIGHT CLIMATE CHANGE WITH YOUR PEN... 112

MISSION COMPLETED.. 114

SUPERHERO POINTS.. 118

WHAT KIND OF SUPERHERO ARE YOU?................................ 124

**FIND OUT MORE ABOUT THE FIGHT AGAINST
CLIMATE CHANGE**.. 126

ABOUT THE AUTHOR AND THE 2 MINUTE FOUNDATION...... 127

ARE YOU READY TO BE A SUPERHERO?

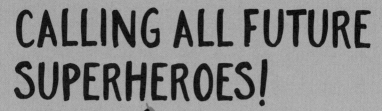

CALLING ALL FUTURE SUPERHEROES!

Hello, you.

How are you fixed for time?

Could you spare two minutes?

Great!

How about taking two minutes to do something really, really amazing?

Like becoming an activist and helping to save the planet.

Would you be up for that?

I knew you would.

WE NEED YOU TO SAVE THE PLANET

Planet Earth needs superheroes to fight climate change. The ideal candidate is YOU! It doesn't matter how tall you are, where you live, or whether you have special powers. You can become a **#2minutesuperhero**, as long as you can do the following:

Job: #2minutesuperhero
Start date: Immediate start
Experience: No previous experience required
Uniform: Not essential, but a cape could be useful
Skills: Loving planet Earth is essential. Being able to make serious things fun will be looked upon favorably.
Role:

- Being kind to animals
- Helping your family and friends
- Completing your missions
- Fighting climate change two minutes at a time
- Saving the world

Planet Earth is currently looking for superheroes to fight climate change.

WHAT IS HAPPENING TO OUR PLANET?

Our climate (the normal yearly and monthly patterns of weather, such as rainfall and temperature) is changing. This is causing our everyday weather to change too, making some places hotter, some drier, and some wetter. Sea levels are rising. Mountain glaciers are shrinking and ice caps are melting faster than ever before. Plants are flowering at different times. Storms, fires, droughts, floods, and heat waves are having a dramatic effect on people, insects, birds, and other animals all across the world.

Some places are becoming difficult for humans and animals to live in because of the change in climate, and if we don't do something about it right now, it's only going to get worse.

HOW WILL A CHANGING CLIMATE AFFECT US?

Think about the weather today. Was it raining, hot, cold, or windy? The weather impacts us every day, whether we realize it or not. We adapt by putting on a sweater if it's cold, a T-shirt if it's warm, or a raincoat if it's wet. But it will be harder to adapt to more extreme changes in the global climate. As a result, we won't be able to continue living our lives the way we do.

HOW WILL A CHANGING CLIMATE AFFECT NATURE?

The weather affects everything on our planet, from the bottom of the oceans to the top of the highest mountains and everything in between. That includes all animals and plants. So when normal weather patterns alter because of climate change, some animals and plants can't adapt quickly enough. Suddenly they do not have enough to eat and drink or places to shelter where they are safe from storms, flooding, or fires. They may be in danger. After a while, their whole species may be in danger too. They could even become extinct. Some are already. Nobody wants that, right?

PENGUIN PROBLEMS: Warming sea temperatures due to climate change are making it harder for African penguins to feed. Young penguins swim thousands of miles, following tiny organisms called plankton. The plankton normally lead them to their favorite food: sardines. But warmer water temperatures mean the sardines have moved to another part of the ocean and the penguins go hungry.

WHAT IS THE CAUSE OF CLIMATE CHANGE?

The Earth's climate has always changed, but over the last eighty years there has been an unexpected increase in the average global temperature. Most scientists are convinced that this is because of human activity. Building factories, driving cars, and flying airplanes all upset the balance of our planet by releasing gases into the Earth's atmosphere. These gases form a blanket around the Earth, trapping heat from the Sun. Over time, the gases cause the planet to warm up and the climate to change in different ways across the world.

Everything we do in our everyday lives has an effect on climate change. The way we eat, travel, heat our homes, use electricity, and shop can either help us to fight it or make it worse. So it's important that you take decisive action now to stop the further warming of the planet, instead of sitting around waiting for someone else to do it.

WHY IT IS UP TO YOU TO FIGHT

Planet Earth is our home, and it's the only one we've got. It's a wonderful place, and we share it with wonderful animals and plants. Anyone who calls planet Earth home has a part to play in saving it because we are all connected. Yes, YOU are related to worms, seaweed, polar bears, and puffins. It might be a very long way back in our family tree, but we all came from the same single-celled blob millions of years ago. As a family, we should look out for one another!

We all need one another in order to live happy lives on Earth. As a human, everything you do has some kind of impact on the planet, which makes you vitally important. That's why, in this book, you'll find a series of missions that will help you understand climate change and what you can do to fight it.

Each mission will change how you think about the way you live your life. Completing a mission will have a positive effect on the planet. And it will make you a **#2minutesuperhero**. After all, doing good deeds is what superheroes are all about. (You got the job, by the way.)

EVERYDAY SUPERHERO

Name: Arrie

Job: Arctic fox

Superpower: Being difficult to see in snow

How climate change affects you: The Arctic is getting warmer. With less snow and sea ice, it's harder to find the food I need to survive.

Top tip: Wear white for camouflage

Hates: Melting ice

Loves: Chasing lemmings

ARRIE

JOIN THE EVERYDAY SUPERHEROES

The planet needs you to become an activist—that's someone who gets off the sofa and does stuff—and join an ever-growing family of everyday superheroes who fight climate change. These real-life superheroes get on with their lives doing simple, everyday things that have a positive effect on the planet. You can find them everywhere, from the polar ice caps to the rainforest and even the street where you live. You're going to meet some of them in this book. I hope they inspire you to be like them.

So while the bad news is that our home is in trouble, the good news is that to make a difference you don't have to outsmart an evil genius or tackle an army of zombies. You just have to be you.

If you have any doubts about whether you're up to it, just think about how you had to change because of the global coronavirus pandemic. If you can do that, you can do this. In fact, you're practically a superhero already!

ME AND MY #2MINUTEMISSION

Before we get started, can I tell you a little bit about myself? My name is Martin. I am an eco-activist, beach cleaner, and writer. I believe that everybody has the power to change the world. And I believe we can do it through small actions, which all add up to make a BIG difference.

My beach litter campaign, the **#2minutebeachclean**, encourages people to pick up plastic for two minutes every day. Two minutes is no time at all, and yet it can really change things, especially once your friends and family get involved!

I realized that we can use the same idea to fight climate change. Every two minutes make a difference! And that's why I'm here: to help you complete your missions and become the very best **#2minutesuperhero** you can be.

⭐ EVERYDAY SUPERHERO ⭐

Name: Martin

Job: Writer and Activist

Superpower: Using words to get people to do good stuff

How you fight climate change: I pick up litter, write books, plant trees, and ride my bike

Top tip: Everybody can make a difference

Hates: Wasting energy

Loves: Solar showers

MARTIN

HOW TO USE THIS BOOK

♣ This book contains a series of **MISSIONS**. Each will help you to understand climate change, what you can do to fight it, and the areas of your life where you **CAN** make a difference.

♣ The big missions all contain **2-MINUTE MISSIONS**. These are tasks that I want you to do. Each task is worth superhero points.

♣ Some of the **2-MINUTE MISSIONS** are hard. Some are easy. The harder missions will earn you more points. Some will also take longer than two minutes!

♣ After you complete a mission, count up the points you have earned and make a note of them.

♣ Once you have finished the book, add up your points to get your final score. Turn to page 124 to find out what kind of superhero you are.

SUPERHERO STAT: Saving the planet can make you happy. And that's the truth.

READY FOR ACTION?

Before you begin your first mission, I need you to pledge your allegiance to planet Earth and all things in it.

I solemnly pledge my allegiance to planet Earth.

I will fight climate change through my actions and will take two minutes of every day to help nature and the natural world.

Training approved by:

Founder of the #2minutebeachclean

THE SUPERHERO'S GUIDE TO LIVING A PLANET-FRIENDLY LIFE

Rip up the rule book! Fighting climate change is a Big Job. It's not going to be easy, and there is a lot to do. But you will never be alone. When you play your part, that will inspire others to play their part too. And that's when we'll start to see the difference!

Help nature.

Learn to cook.

Travel under your own steam.

Don't waste food.

WHY THE FIGHT MATTERS

Your first question might be: Why do we need to fight? It's a good question! Although we might not always be able to see climate change happening in front of our eyes, scientists know that it is happening, right here, right now. Lots of animal and plant species are already under threat as a result. If one species is affected, other species that depend on it for food or to spread their seeds are at risk too. We need to keep the world in balance.

EVERY LIVING THING IS VITAL TO PLANET EARTH

All plants, insects, birds, and other animals have a part to play on planet Earth. No species is too small to be important.

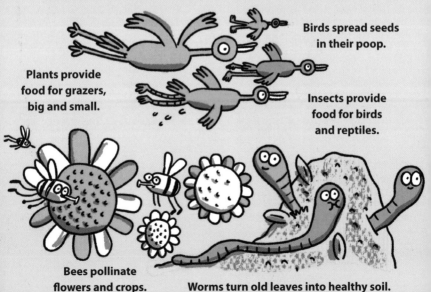

Birds spread seeds in their poop.

Plants provide food for grazers, big and small.

Insects provide food for birds and reptiles.

Bees pollinate flowers and crops.

Worms turn old leaves into healthy soil.

THE WORLD HANGS IN THE BALANCE

Our world is made up of many different ecosystems. An ecosystem is a group of living things in a certain area that interact with one another and with nonliving things, such as water, soil, and the climate. Ecosystems come in different sizes and can be anything from the entire planet to a coral reef, a grassland, or that old tree trunk in your local park. Anything that happens within an ecosystem is important, because everything depends on everything else in a carefully balanced way.

In the African bush ecosystem, for example, elephants trample down plants, creating space for trees to grow. Elephants eat the plants, then poop out the seeds. Those seeds become new plants and provide a home and food for all kinds of animals. If you remove the elephants from the bush ecosystem, everything changes. No elephant poop = no plants or trees = no homes or food for other living things.

⭐ EVERYDAY SUPERHERO ⭐

Name: Nellie

Job: African elephant

Superpower: My incredible trunk

How climate change affects you: Droughts will make it harder for me to find water to drink

Top tip: I spread seeds in my poop

Hates: Competing with humans for space to live

Loves: Playing in water

NELLIE

21

WHAT HAPPENS WHEN BALANCE IS LOST?

Problems occur when the changing climate—or another factor such as the loss of habitat or pollution—upsets the balance of an ecosystem. The species that live there might not have the food, water, or shelter they need to survive. Giant pandas, for example, eat lots of bamboo. If climate change affects the rate of bamboo growth, panda numbers may fall.

When the last animal of a certain type dies, that species becomes extinct and will never be seen again. You might have heard of the dodo or the Tasmanian tiger. They became extinct years ago. Now you can only see a dodo by going to a museum. That's no good, is it?

Did you know that in a single year (2019), more than a dozen animals, including three bird species, a small mammal, and a species of snail, became extinct? They will never be seen again. If you needed a reason to FIGHT, this is it!

THE GOOD NEWS!

Don't despair! There are ways that we can help fight extinction. Take the example of the Eurasian beaver, which had disappeared from Britain by the sixteenth century due to overhunting. Well, now the beaver is back! Thanks to careful conservation efforts, the beaver has been reintroduced to several sites across Britain, including Scotland and Devon. Beavers build dams, create new ecosystems, and help stop flooding. Those brilliant, busy beavers!

WE MUST FIGHT FOR US TOO!

We all play a part in the planet's ecosystem. Humans are smart. But we can't survive on our own. We need nature! Without healthy soil to grow the plants we eat, bees to pollinate our crops, plankton to feed the fish we catch, and forests to give us the oxygen we breathe, we will have nothing. The destruction of ecosystems has also been shown to lead to more disease outbreaks among human populations. We have to act, and act now. It's our duty as superheroes, right?

THE BAD NEWS: More than 32,000 species are in danger of extinction.

41% OF AMPHIBIANS
26% OF MAMMALS
14% OF BIRDS
ARE FACING EXTINCTION!

THE EFFECTS OF CLIMATE CHANGE

OK, superheroes! Now that we know why we need to fight climate change, it's time to look in more detail at the things that are happening as a result of it. Some of this is scary, and some of it is sad. But don't be put off. Across the world, people are coming together to fight it.

IS CLIMATE CHANGE REAL?

Some people will tell you that climate change isn't real. Perhaps they don't understand it, are frightened of change, or make money from damaging the planet.

Ninety-seven percent of climate scientists agree that it is real and that it is caused by human activity. It is VERY unlikely the scientists are wrong. But what if you complete all your missions, and things turn out not to be as bad as feared?

What if you plant more trees, travel by bike, walk to school with your friends, look after bees, encourage animals and birds to live in your garden, eat fresh and tasty local food, make less waste, and wear lovely, sustainable clothes, and it's all for nothing?

Well, you'll have saved money, spent time with friends, discovered wildlife, enjoyed a healthy lifestyle, and stayed warm and stylish. Doesn't sound too bad, does it?

HOW FAST IS THE CLIMATE CHANGING?

The global climate has always varied as the planet heats up and cools down. But now the average temperature of the planet is steadily increasing. By the end of this century, scientists think that temperatures could increase by 5–9°F (3–5°C).

According to data from NASA, 2016 was the warmest year since 1880. The ten warmest years in the 140-year record have all occurred since 2005.

GLOBAL AVERAGE TEMPERATURE

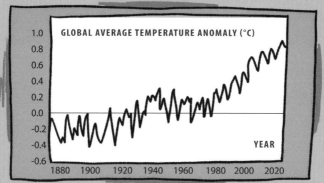

At the time this book was written, 2020 was the second-warmest year on record. The global temperature was 2°F (1.1°C) warmer than the average for 1850–1900, which was a period when many factories were just being built during the Industrial Revolution.

As the planet heats up, the weather is also getting more extreme. Scientists have noticed:

♣ ice caps, ice sheets, and glaciers are melting
♣ sea levels are rising
♣ oceans are warming and becoming more acidic
♣ rain patterns are changing
♣ heat waves are more common
♣ hurricanes and storms are more frequent

25

WHAT ARE THE EFFECTS OF CLIMATE CHANGE ON NATURE?

It sounds kind of great to have warmer temperatures, doesn't it? We all like hot, sunny days.

But there's more to it than that.

While we've had mini ice ages and warmer periods, the temperature on Earth has been relatively stable for thousands of years, and living things have adapted accordingly.

The climate determines where the deserts are, where the rain falls, when the ice melts, and what time of year the trees and flowers bloom. Species have adapted to their environments. Bees are brilliant at pollinating plants. Polar bears have gotten good at living on ice caps. Penguins are excellent at surviving in Antarctic seas. Carefully balanced ecosystems can be found across the world, from icy mountaintops to coral reefs in the ocean.

Now as global temperatures rise, ecosystems cannot always stay balanced. They might become hotter, wetter, or drier. This in turn causes plants, insects, birds, and other animals to lose their food sources or homes.

TURTLEY UNBELIEVABLE: Climate change can have an effect on turtles. An increase in sand temperatures at their nesting sites can affect the sex of their young.

ICE-FREE: The Arctic could be ice-free in the summer by 2050 based on the current rate of climate change.

It now takes longer for the sea to freeze in winter, so there is less time for polar bears to hunt seals on the ice.

Mountaintop species are moving farther up the slopes to find cooler temperatures to live in.

Warmer seas leave coral reefs at risk of bleaching, which is when they lose their color and die.

Bumblebee numbers have fallen dramatically in North America and Europe.

⭐ **EVERYDAY SUPERHERO** ⭐

Name: Peter

Job: Polar bear

Superpower: Surviving on polar ice

How climate change affects you: My home is melting! I need ice to hunt for my dinner.

Top tip: Learn to swim

Hates: Eating out of garbage bins

Loves: Creeping up on seals

PETER

WHAT ARE THE EFFECTS OF CLIMATE CHANGE ON US?

Hey! I need you to read this. Don't be scared. Instead, let this knowledge inspire you to finish all the missions in this book. Let it be the light that guides you. You can make a difference.

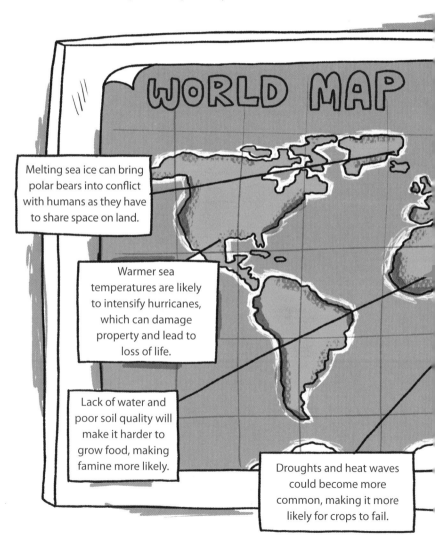

Melting sea ice can bring polar bears into conflict with humans as they have to share space on land.

Warmer sea temperatures are likely to intensify hurricanes, which can damage property and lead to loss of life.

Lack of water and poor soil quality will make it harder to grow food, making famine more likely.

Droughts and heat waves could become more common, making it more likely for crops to fail.

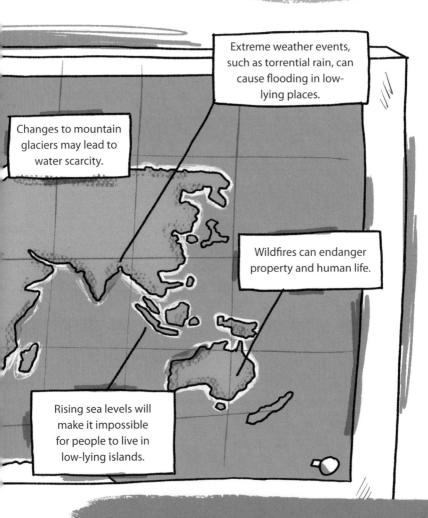

Extreme weather events, such as torrential rain, can cause flooding in low-lying places.

Changes to mountain glaciers may lead to water scarcity.

Wildfires can endanger property and human life.

Rising sea levels will make it impossible for people to live in low-lying islands.

YOUR MISSIONS START NOW . . .

COUNT YOUR CARBON

In our first mission, we are going to look at the science behind climate change. If we can understand why the global temperature is increasing, we can understand how to fight it and why the things you do in just two minutes matter. Let's do this!

THE GREENHOUSE EFFECT

The Earth is surrounded by a layer of gases, including oxygen and nitrogen, known as the atmosphere. The atmosphere also contains small amounts of what scientists call "greenhouse gases." These include carbon dioxide and methane.

Greenhouse gases get their name because they act like the glass in a greenhouse. During the day, the Sun warms the Earth's surface, and at night the heat is released back into the atmosphere. The greenhouse gases trap some of this heat and help keep the planet at a stable temperature, one that's warm enough for living things to survive, but not too hot.

So far, so good! But the problem has come when human activity has increased the amounts of greenhouse gases in our atmosphere. Carbon dioxide is released when humans burn gasoline, aviation fuel, or coal. Methane, another greenhouse gas, is released when cows on meat or dairy farms fart or burp (among other things). The more greenhouse gases that humans release into the atmosphere, the more heat is trapped, which in turn raises the average global temperature.

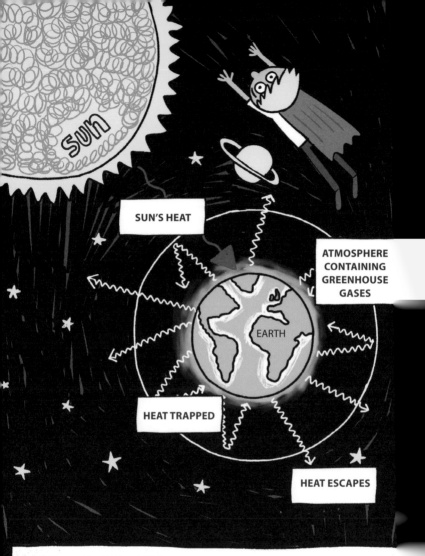

SUN'S HEAT

ATMOSPHERE CONTAINING GREENHOUSE GASES

EARTH

HEAT TRAPPED

HEAT ESCAPES

YOUR 2-MINUTE MISSION: Next time it's sunny, find a greenhouse or a room with a big window. When the light shines through the glass, what happens to the temperature inside? If you can find a thermometer, measure the temperature outside and inside and calculate the difference.
5 POINTS

REDUCING GREENHOUSE GASES

To fight climate change, we need to slow the rise of the average global temperature. To make that happen, we have to start living our lives in ways that reduce the amount of greenhouse gases we produce. That means cutting down on our activities that give out, or emit, carbon dioxide and methane.

WHERE DOES CARBON DIOXIDE COME FROM?

Carbon is one of the building blocks of our planet. Almost everything has carbon in it: you, me, trees, animals, and your sneakers. When things change—a tree grows, you breathe, or a pair of new sneakers gets delivered to your door—carbon is either stored or released into the atmosphere. When it is released into the atmosphere, it combines with oxygen to form an invisible gas known as carbon dioxide (often written as CO_2).

- ♠ Humans and animals breathe in oxygen from the atmosphere and breathe out carbon dioxide.
- ♠ Human activities that involve burning fuel, like driving a car or flying in an airplane, also release carbon dioxide into the atmosphere.
- ♠ Trees and plants take in carbon dioxide and store it as carbon in their leaves. Oceans store it via plankton. They then release oxygen into the atmosphere.

SUPER BREATH: In one day, the average superhero breathes out about 2.2 pounds (1 kilogram) of CO_2.

TREEMENDOUS: One tree can absorb around 48 pounds (21 kilograms) of CO_2 in a year.

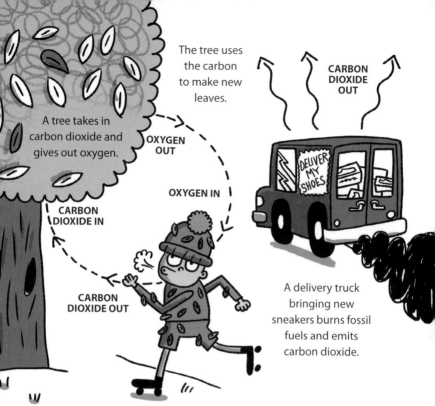

The tree uses the carbon to make new leaves.

CARBON DIOXIDE OUT

A tree takes in carbon dioxide and gives out oxygen.

OXYGEN OUT

OXYGEN IN

CARBON DIOXIDE IN

CARBON DIOXIDE OUT

A delivery truck bringing new sneakers burns fossil fuels and emits carbon dioxide.

Humans and animals breathe in oxygen and breathe out carbon dioxide.

FOSSIL FUELS AND CARBON DIOXIDE

One of the main causes of climate change is the way we create energy by burning fossil fuels. Fossil fuels, which include coal, gas, and oil, formed deep in the Earth from the remains of plants and organisms that died millions of years ago and were then subjected to high temperatures and huge pressure over a very long time. We extract the fossil fuels from the ground and burn them to make electricity, heat our homes, and power our vehicles. The problem is that fossil fuels are rich in carbon, and burning them releases their stored carbon into the atmosphere as carbon dioxide gas.

FOSSIL FUELS AND US

Fossil fuels have changed the way we live our lives over the last two hundred years, making our days brighter, warmer, and easier. However, the catch is that whether we like it or not, every activity we do has an associated carbon cost: it either stores carbon or releases carbon dioxide.

At the moment, we are burning fossil fuels at a rate that releases more carbon dioxide into the atmosphere than the plants, oceans, and forests can store. We need to slow down!

LOCKDOWN LIFE: In early April 2020, during the lockdowns caused by the coronavirus pandemic, carbon dioxide emissions across the world fell by 17 percent compared to the same period in 2019.

YOUR CARBON FOOTPRINT

Your carbon footprint is the amount of carbon you release into the atmosphere in your daily life. Everything you do impacts your footprint. That includes how you heat your house, what you eat, what you buy, whether you recycle, and how you get to school.

Every choice you make affects the footprint you leave on the Earth. Think of it like footsteps on sand. If you tread lightly, you hardly leave a footprint. If you walk with heavy steps, you will disturb the sand.

YOUR 2-MINUTE MISSION: Think about your carbon footprint. Can you come up with one small action you could do tomorrow to reduce it?
10 POINTS

THE AVERAGE SUPERHERO'S CARBON FOOTPRINT

The average climate change–fighting superhero lives a thoughtful life, trying to make as little impact as possible on the planet. Their carbon footprint isn't zero, because that's almost impossible. But it is small. They walk instead of getting a ride. They don't waste food or energy, and they always turn off the tap when they brush their teeth.

Read the next few chapters and you'll understand why.

But until then, go lightly. YOU CAN DO IT!

MISSION 2
YOU'VE GOT THE POWER

Now that you know why we're fighting, it's time to start on the real work. We're going to begin with energy. Energy usage is simple: the more we use, the more impact it has on the planet. And if we want to reduce our carbon footprint, we need to look carefully at what kind of energy we use and how we generate it.

WHAT DOES ENERGY DO?

Energy is the stuff that makes you go whiz, bang, and pop! It's the puff in your run and the oomph in the car, the clickety-clack in the train and the ahhh in your bath. It's the zoom in your cereal and the music in your radio, the wow in your phone and the light in your life. Energy makes things happen!

We use energy to produce toys.

We use energy to see.

We use energy to cook.

We use energy to travel.

HOW WE POWER OUR LIVES TODAY

For us, living in our world, energy is mostly electricity: the fizz in our plugs. It is the juice that runs your TV, charges your phone, turns on the lights, washes the clothes, heats your bathwater, keeps your fridge cold, makes sweet music, and runs our factories, shops, and schools. But where does that energy come from?

Electrical energy is created in power plants that form the country's electricity system. It runs as a current through wires that go from the power plants to our homes.

We're clever enough to get electricity from lots of sources. Some of those sources are renewable, which means there will always be more of them, while others are nonrenewable, which means one day they will run out. Some energy sources are better for the planet than others because they don't emit greenhouse gases or pollution.

YOUR 2-MINUTE MISSION: **THINK ENERGY! Think about what you've done today. Did it use energy? What kinds of energy did it use?**
10 POINTS

NONRENEWABLE ENERGY

Nonrenewable sources of energy will all be used up one day.

There is a limited supply of fossil fuels. They take millions of years to form, and we are using them up faster than they are produced. Oil, coal, and gas are fossil fuels. Once they are extracted from the ground, we burn them to make heat and electricity, or as fuel that powers cars, ships, and airplanes.

The process of burning fossil fuels releases heat, water, carbon dioxide, and other pollution. As a result, fossil fuels are known as "dirty energy."

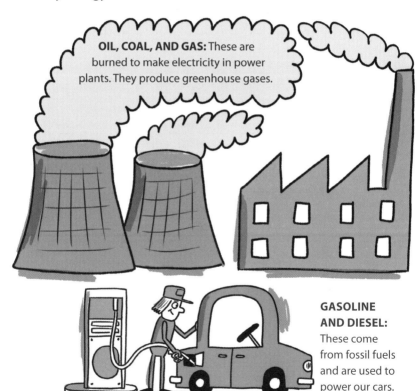

OIL, COAL, AND GAS: These are burned to make electricity in power plants. They produce greenhouse gases.

GASOLINE AND DIESEL: These come from fossil fuels and are used to power our cars.

RENEWABLE ENERGY

The great news is that fossil fuels aren't the only way we can produce energy. There are plenty of options for us to get our energy from renewable sources. That means they can be replaced and will not run out. These sources of energy don't release greenhouse gases or other pollution into the atmosphere. They are sometimes known as "clean" or "green" energy.

WIND: This can be used to make turbines turn and create electricity.

SUN: Solar panels can be used to make electricity and heat water.

WATER: This can be used to power turbines to make electricity.

GEOTHERMAL: Hot water and steam from deep underground can be used to turn turbines.

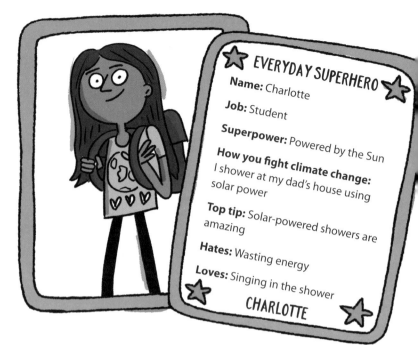

THE MIRACLE OF SOLAR POWER

The Sun's power is FREE. Energy from solar power doesn't create any greenhouse gas emissions and won't ever run out, which is why it could be the very best form of power for the future. Even in areas that aren't very sunny, solar power can provide enough power to light up our homes. To be able to convert the Sun's energy into electricity to run your home or to store its heat to warm up your shower, you need solar panels.

SUNSHINE FACT:

China is the country with the most solar power. Approximately 3 percent of its total power comes from the Sun.

MAKE POWER FROM WATER

Water power—or hydroelectric power—is another source of clean energy. It uses the energy from moving water to turn the turbines (electric motors in reverse) that make electricity.

WATERNAMAZING FACT: Norway gets 95 percent of its power from hydroelectric energy. They have a lot of water in Norway! In the US only about 7 percent of our energy comes from water.

USING THE WIND

We can also use the power of the wind. When it blows, you'll see the blades of tall wind turbines turning, which generates electricity. The turbines can be found in windy spots or out in the ocean. Wind is a clean, efficient energy source that won't ever run out. Isn't that amazing?

WINDY FACT: In the US, around 8.4 percent of our energy is produced by wind. That's enough to power more than 34 million homes!

YOUR 2-MINUTE MISSION: Where does your energy come from? Some companies offer electricity from renewable sources. Talk to your parents or caregivers about it. 30 POINTS

FIGHT CLIMATE CHANGE AT HOME

Climate change is a funny thing. You can't see it as you walk to school or as you play in the park. It may seem difficult to fight, like an enemy that keeps shifting its shape.

But the thing is that climate change is happening because of things we do in our homes and schools and on our days out. The best way we can tackle it is to start at home. Your home! And it's as simple as turning off the lights.

MAKE YOUR MISSIONS FUN

I am going to admit something to you now. Fighting climate change isn't always exciting. But your job as a superhero is to make your missions fun. How? You decide. Look at it with your special superhero vision (it is a thing, trust me) and give it a go. Make games for your family. Draw pictures. Make people smile and feel proud of what they've achieved. Because every single thing you do in this fight matters.

HOME TRUTHS:

In 2018, around 20 percent of all carbon emissions in the US were generated by heating, lighting, cooking, and charging our phones.

STAND BY ME

When you leave the house or go to bed, how many of your devices or appliances get left on standby? The TV? Your computer? Your video game console? A printer? Devices left on standby still use energy, even though you aren't using them. It's time to become the energy police!

You can cut down on your carbon footprint by getting an adult to unplug any devices you usually leave on standby. If the device is off, it won't be using energy, so you will also save your family money!

YOUR 2-MINUTE MISSION: **Count up the rooms in your house where there are devices that are regularly left on standby. Make a sign for each one that says: NOT IN USE? CUT THE JUICE! 20 POINTS**

TURN IF OFF

Do people in your family leave the lights on when they're the last one to leave a room? *Grrrr!* Every light left on unnecessarily is wasting energy.

YOUR 2-MINUTE MISSION: **Make a chart with the name of each family member on it. Every time someone turns off a light when they leave a room, give them a gold star. Who is the most energy-efficient? 10 POINTS**

FIGHT CLIMATE CHANGE WITH A SWEATER

One of the biggest ways we use energy in our homes is to keep us warm. Our household heating is responsible for a lot of carbon emissions. So the more you can turn it down—or even avoid turning it on at all—the better!

SHUT THAT DOOR!

YOUR 2-MINUTE MISSION: **Close doors when you leave a room—this will stop heat from escaping.**
5 POINTS

IT'S CURTAINS FOR YOU OR THE PLANET!

YOUR 2-MINUTE MISSION: **Close curtains at night to keep heat in.**
5 POINTS

SUPERHEROES WEAR SWEATERS!

YOUR 2-MINUTE MISSION: **Put on a sweater—not the heat—if you feel a bit chilly.**
5 POINTS

SNUGGLE LIKE A BOSS!

YOUR 2-MINUTE MISSION: Use an extra blanket on your bed instead of turning up the heat.
5 POINTS

PUT A SOCK ON IT!

YOUR 2-MINUTE MISSION: Get some woolly socks or superhero slippers to put on when you come home from school so you don't get cold feet.
5 POINTS

SWITCH IT OFF FOR LONGER!

YOUR 2-MINUTE MISSION: Does your heating go on and off at set times? Ask your parents or caregivers if you can change the settings slightly. An hour less a day will make a difference!
10 POINTS

BAN THE BINGE

Watching TV creates greenhouse gases. And more so if you binge shows online. Why? Because it takes energy to access the Internet and for your device to talk to other computers in order to stream the show. If your family is using the Internet to watch different programs at the same time, you will use more energy than if you watch together.

> YOUR 2-MINUTE MISSION: **Watch your favorite programs together instead of separately, as if you were at the movies, with popcorn and goodies. It'll be fun, and it will help save the planet too!**
> **10 POINTS**

RECYCLE FOR PLANET EARTH

Did you know that recycling is good for the planet? The less you put into the trash, the better. Throwing away glass, plastic, and metal means we just have to use energy to make the same materials all over again. And that's bad. So the more we can reuse and recycle the stuff we've already got, the smaller our carbon footprints will be.

RECYCLE: Get to know what can be recycled and what can't.

REPAIR: Old stuff that's broken can be fixed and given away instead of being thrown out.

REDUCE: Can you help your family reduce the size of their weekly trash bag?

REFILL: Old glass jars can be washed and then refilled. Plastic containers can also be reused, but not for drinking.

REUSE: Don't throw it away. Use reusable face masks that you wash after each use.

> **YOUR 2-MINUTE MISSION: Put yourself in charge of the recycling in your house. You are king or queen of collection day. Make sure all your recycling is ready to go into the right bin.**
> **10 POINTS**

FIGHT CLIMATE CHANGE WITH YOUR FOOD

Food is vital to you, me, everyone, and everything on the planet. Trees need water and sunlight, otters need fish, and we need our lunch. Without it, we—and they—can't go about our day-to-day lives. Otters can be grumpy when they get hungry. Just saying.

Having enough food for everyone on planet Earth is going to be a challenge as the human population increases. We know we need to produce more food. How we do this is important, because food production contributes to climate change. We need to think carefully about what we eat, and if we can make changes, we should!

EATING HEALTHILY FOR YOU AND THE PLANET

Everyone needs a balanced diet to grow up healthy and strong. Eat well and your body will thank you. However, it's important for superheroes to know that what they put on their plate affects the planet. Some methods of producing crops and raising livestock create more carbon emissions than others, so your diet does make a difference to your carbon footprint. You don't need to make massive changes to how you eat (unless you want to), but there are lots of small changes your family can consider. Let's start by thinking about what might be on your plate.

OMNIVORE: You eat fish, meat, and animal-based products, as well as plants. You might just eat fish and no meat.

VEGETARIAN: You don't eat fish or meat, in favor of a plant-based diet. You eat animal-based products such as milk, eggs, cheese, and honey.

VEGAN: You don't eat any animal-based products, including dairy, eggs, and honey, in favor of a plant-based diet.

DOES EATING MEAT AND DAIRY AFFECT THE PLANET?

Some people believe that cutting down—or cutting out—meat and dairy is one of the most effective actions you can take to fight climate change. Why? Raising livestock requires land, so forests are cut down for farmland. The animals need food to eat and water to drink and therefore use a lot of resources that take energy to produce. And when certain animals—such as cows— fart, they produce methane, which is a greenhouse gas.

WHY CUT DOWN ON MEAT AND DAIRY?

✦ Intensive animal farming requires land for the animals. This leads to a loss of ecosystems.

✦ Rainforests are being cut down to create space to grow crops to feed farm animals.

✦ Livestock farming uses lots of water.

✦ Cow burps, farts, and poop give off methane, which is a greenhouse gas.

✦ A glass of dairy milk results in almost three times more greenhouse gas emissions than a plant-based milk.

EAT LOCAL

If you eat meat, it's worth thinking about where your meat has come from. Meat that has been reared near where you live will have a lower carbon footprint than meat that has traveled thousands of miles to your plate. Wherever possible, eat local. What the animal has been fed will also play a part in its carbon footprint. If it has been fed on grass (beef or lamb) or grain (chicken), it will be better for the planet than if it has been fed on soybeans grown in South American rainforests.

WHY CHOOSE LOCAL MEAT?

♠ It has a lower carbon footprint than meat from far away.

♠ Grass-fed meat allows us to get nutrients from land that couldn't be used for anything else.

♠ Well-managed grazing farmland can be effective at storing carbon.

YOUR 2-MINUTE MISSION: If you're a meat lover, ask your family if you can go one day without eating any meat at all. It's a simple thing, but it will make a difference, especially if you make it a weekly thing.
20 POINTS

FISHY ON A DISHY

Eating fish can also affect the planet. Fish play an important role in ocean ecosystems, and now some fish are facing extinction because of overfishing. Others are caught in wasteful ways, when, for example, a larger species, like a dolphin, gets caught in nets intended to catch smaller fish, like tuna. Another negative impact of fishing is that the nets and equipment create lots of plastic waste, which harms ocean wildlife. So next time you are digging into your fish fingers and fries, take two minutes to think about how your fish has arrived on your dish!

YOUR 2-MINUTE MISSION: **Check the database of the Monterey Bay Aquarium Seafood Watch (www.seafoodwatch.org) to see if the fish you eat regularly is environmentally sustainable. Can you either cut it out or switch to a more ocean-friendly option if it scores poorly? 20 POINTS**

PLANT POWER

You may already be a
vegetarian or considering
trying it. The most important
thing is that you eat a balanced
diet and stay healthy, so remember to talk to your parents or
caregivers before making any changes.

Vegetarians get their energy from a plant-based diet.
Growing crops takes up less land and water than raising
animals for meat or dairy and so puts less pressure on the
environment. It also reduces your carbon footprint and
greenhouse gas emissions.

YOUR 2-MINUTE MISSION: **Next time you have the
option to choose veggies over meat (your packed-
lunch sandwich filling, your school-lunch choice,
your after-school snack), say yes to plant power!
20 POINTS**

GOING VEGAN

Being vegan means your diet is entirely plant-based. You don't eat meat or fish or animal-based products such as cheese, milk, yogurt, eggs, or honey. The welfare of animals is a big reason why people go vegan, as is the fact that eating zero animal-based products reduces the impact we have on the planet.

There are lots of vegan alternatives that you can eat to ensure that you have a balanced diet. These include milk, cheese, butter, and meat alternatives that you can swap into your meals. Before changing, you will need to talk to your parents or caregivers and carefully plan to make sure you are getting all the energy you need to perform your superhero deeds!

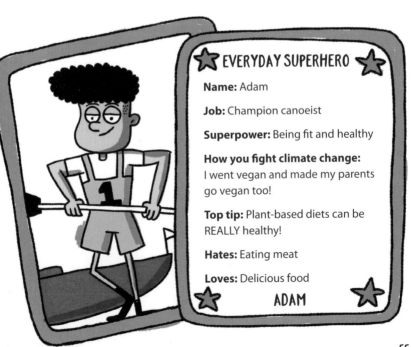

⭐ EVERYDAY SUPERHERO ⭐

Name: Adam

Job: Champion canoeist

Superpower: Being fit and healthy

How you fight climate change: I went vegan and made my parents go vegan too!

Top tip: Plant-based diets can be REALLY healthy!

Hates: Eating meat

Loves: Delicious food

ADAM

THE IMPACT OF PLANTS

While eating a plant-based diet is fantastic for the planet, there are still things to consider when choosing your alternative. People are switching from cow's milk to alternative milks to cut down on their carbon emissions, but some crops that we use for meat or dairy substitutes—like soy, quinoa, and almonds—actually have a high carbon footprint, and their packaging is hard to recycle.

OAT MILK

ALMOND MILK

SOY MILK

Pros: We already grow lots of oats, so rainforests don't need to be cut down to plant them.

Cons: Oats can be sprayed with harmful chemicals.

Pros: It doesn't require as much land to grow as other milk alternatives.

Cons: Almonds require lots of water to grow, and the production methods are bad for bees.

Pros: It offers a similar amount of energy compared to cow's milk.

Cons: Rainforests are cut down to grow soybeans.

YOUR 2-MINUTE MISSION: **Try a milk alternative on your breakfast cereal. Think about where the alternative is grown and how it is packaged. Can it be recycled?**
10 POINTS

WHY COOKING AT HOME IS GREAT

Whatever your diet preferences, making dishes from scratch can be better for you and better for the planet than buying prepared meals or individual portions. And you can cut down on your plastic waste too! It may take more time to prepare home-cooked food than to pop a frozen meal in the microwave or order takeout, but it doesn't have to be more expensive. If you can help your parents or caregivers cook one homemade meal a week, you will be boosting your health—and the planet's! Look in your library for cool recipe books for superheroes (kids like you) and see what options will work for your family!

LOVE YOUR LEFTOVERS

Throwing food away is really bad for the planet, not only because it wastes food (which took energy to grow), but also because it takes energy to dispose of it. Collecting your household waste and then disposing of it all emits greenhouse gases. So eat up those greens! In fact, fight food waste by eating up everything on your plate!

YOUR 2-MINUTE MISSION: **If you can't finish your dinner, rather than toss it, pop it in a container and save it for a snack or dinner the next day. Cold pizza is great, and curries and chili are always better on day two. FACT! 5 POINTS**

FIGHT CLIMATE CHANGE WITH YOUR SINK, SHOWER, AND TOILET

How we use water in our daily lives is part of our energy consumption. Cleaning and filtering water so it's safe to drink, pumping it to our homes, and heating it so we can wash all require electricity.

I'm not saying we should stop bathing, drinking, or washing our clothes. No one likes a stinky superhero. But the less water we use, the more we can reduce our carbon footprint and the better it is for the planet! It's showers only from now on. And make them snappy!

HOW WATER USAGE AFFECTS CLIMATE CHANGE

The more wisely you use water, the more you help the planet.

WASHING DISHES: It takes energy to heat water for washing dishes or running a dishwasher.

WASHING CLOTHES: Washing machines heat water to wash clothes.

FLUSHING THE TOILET: Toilets make up about 30 percent of the water we use.

WASHING YOU: Heating water to shower or bathe uses energy.

THINK BEFORE YOU FLUSH

Toilets can waste a lot of water. Adjusting them to use less can save hundreds of gallons of water a year, which in turn reduces your carbon footprint and lowers your bills.

With the help of your parents or caregivers, you can make a device that will save water—and money—every time you flush. Double win!

THROWING IT DOWN THE DRAIN: Every toilet flush takes 1.6 gallons (6 liters) of water. So a family of four may use more than 9,200 gallons (35,000 liters) of water each year. Just to flush the toilet!

YOU WILL NEED:
A small, clean plastic bottle (a one-quart milk container or 16-ounce drink bottle); clean stones.

1. With the help of a parent or caregiver, cut the top off your bottle.
2. Take the lid off your toilet tank and place the bottle in the corner. It must not touch any of the toilet's working parts.
3. Fill the bottle with the stones to weigh it down.
4. Flush the toilet and allow the tank to fill up, making sure the bottle fills up too.
5. Now flush and see that the bottle stays full. That will be the amount of water you save each time you flush!
6. Replace the lid on the tank.

**YOUR 2-MINUTE MISSION: Make a water-saving device for your toilet tank with your parents or caregivers.
20 POINTS**

DON'T WALLOW: Showering uses up less water than taking a bath, so shower instead of wallowing in the tub!

SHOWER QUICKER: What are you doing in there? Showering for half the time saves half the water.

TURN OFF THE TAP: If you don't already do this, start now. Turn off the tap while you brush your teeth and save water. So simple, and yet it helps save the planet.

WASH IT COOL: Get involved in the laundry! Wash your clothes on the cold setting instead of warm or hot. It saves on the energy needed to heat up the water.

FILL IT UP: Filling the dishwasher so it's full before you switch it on saves water and electricity. And it saves money too! Get involved and stack it for the planet. It will help your family AND get you to superhero status sooner! WIN-WIN.

YOUR 2-MINUTE MISSION: **Do one of these water-saving activities each day. 5 POINTS EACH**

FIGHT CLIMATE CHANGE WITH YOUR (LACK OF) STUFF

How much stuff have you got?
How much of it do you use?
How much of it do you need?
If you're anything like the ten-year-olds in one survey, then you'll have, on average, 238 toys. And you'll play with just twelve of them regularly. Whaaaat!? It might be time to love the planet and cut down on the stuff you own.

WHY HAVING TOO MUCH STUFF CAN BE BAD FOR THE PLANET

Everything that you own—toys, games, instruments, sports equipment—has a carbon footprint that consists of the energy and materials required to make the item, the energy it cost to transport it to you, and the energy it will take to dispose of it. If it's got electronics or a battery inside, or if it is made from plastic, it's in danger of causing pollution when you throw it away. It's a problem. But I know just what to do about it!

> **YOUR 2-MINUTE MISSION: Spread all your toys over your bedroom floor. Pick out the ones you have used in the last few months. Put them in one pile. Put the rest, including stuff that's broken or missing parts, in another pile.**
> **5 POINTS**

HOW TO GET RID OF YOUR UNWANTED STUFF

That pile of stuff that you no longer play with might be useless to you. But it could be useful for someone else. So whatever you do, don't throw it away! Here are four easy missions for making sure your old stuff finds a great new home.

YOUR 2-MINUTE MISSION: **Donate your toys to a charity shop and help raise money for a good cause.**
10 POINTS

YOUR 2-MINUTE MISSION: **Donate your toys to a toy drive so other kids can play with them for free.**
10 POINTS

YOUR 2-MINUTE MISSION: **Give away your old toys to children who are younger than you and will love playing with them.**
10 POINTS

YOUR 2-MINUTE MISSION: **Hold a garage sale and sell toys you don't use.**
10 POINTS

AVOID GETTING MORE STUFF

When do you get stuff? Do you buy it with your allowance? Or do you get most of it at holidays and birthdays? Perhaps you get rewards for doing well at school or for helping around the house.

It's nice to get presents or buy ourselves little treats, especially if we've worked hard to save up the cash. But how about changing the kinds of presents you get or what you spend your money on so it's not all about stuff? How about spending your birthday money or allowance on something fun, such as an amazing day out?

WHY EXPERIENCES ARE BETTER THAN THINGS

Stuff can't give you a smile that lasts for weeks or a giddy feeling in your tummy. It can't get you winded from running or make your sides ache from laughing so much. And it definitely can't make you happy like experiences can.

It might be exciting when you open a present or buy something, but that feeling never lasts. Sliding down a water slide, riding your bike, eating yummy food, and spending time with people you love can make you feel safer, warmer, and happier than stuff ever could.

Visiting a park with your friends will be much better than building one with an app on your tablet. And going for a day out with your family to a fantastic museum is always more interesting than a shelf full of dusty collectible figures.

YOUR 2-MINUTE MISSION: Next time you get asked about what you would like for your birthday, think about the activities you love to do. Suggest an experience rather than more stuff.
20 POINTS

TOP EXPERIENCES

1. How about a day spent learning how to skateboard or play the guitar?
2. How about going to a museum or gallery?
3. How about asking for a day out to see a local sports team play?
4. How about going to the movies or to see a play?

FIGHT CLIMATE CHANGE WITH YOUR GADGETS

Do you have a phone? You might not. But I bet your parents or caregivers do! And I bet you have some sort of device. I am talking about laptops, tablets, game consoles, electronic toys, games, or gadgets. The bad news is that they can all be harmful to the planet. But they needn't be, if you use them carefully.

GADGET POWER

All electrical items use electricity and therefore have a carbon footprint, even when they are on standby or sleep mode. Unplugging them when you are not using them is a great way to fight climate change. Simple!

If your gadget is battery-powered, consider switching to rechargeable batteries that can be reused rather than thrown away after one use.

> YOUR 2-MINUTE MISSION: Ask a parent or caregiver if you can unplug a gadget that isn't used regularly but is left on standby.
> 5 POINTS

YOU DON'T NEED THE NEWEST GADGET

Gadgets are great. But there's always a new one to buy! Each upgrade is responsible for more greenhouse gases being released when the gadget is made, then transported to your home—and when the old one is thrown away.

So how can you fight climate change with your gadgets? Keep the ones you have for as long as you can. Love them. Play with them. Use them. But what if you fall out of love with them or they break? Follow the chart below for some answers.

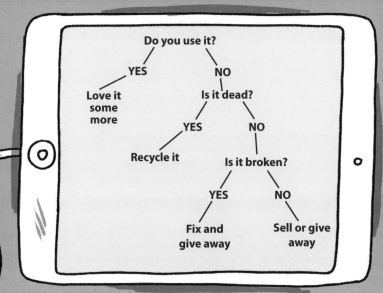

Do you use it?

YES → **Love it some more**

NO → **Is it dead?**

YES → **Recycle it**

NO → **Is it broken?**

YES → **Fix and give away**

NO → **Sell or give away**

YOUR 2-MINUTE MISSION: Go through your old gadgets. If they don't work, see if they can be repaired. If they can't, then recycle them. If they work, give them away or ask a parent or caregiver to help you sell them.
20 POINTS

FIGHT CLIMATE CHANGE WITH YOUR WARDROBE

What are #2minutesuperheroes wearing around town this year? Are you sporting a cape? Underwear on the outside? Mask and bunny slippers? I bet you look dashing.

But did you know that your wardrobe can make a huge difference to climate change? Isn't that amazing? Just by pulling on a different sweater you can fight climate change! Are you ready for this most important of missions?

FUNNY FASHION

Fashion is a funny business. It's a huge global industry that makes billions of dollars each year and relies on being able to quickly sell clothes to you, me, and your family—whether you need them or not. Items come into fashion and then go out of fashion, and because we always want to be in fashion, there's an almost-constant demand for new clothes.

The trouble with this is that it's using up resources more quickly than planet Earth can replace them.

WATER HORROR: It takes 700 gallons (2,700 liters) of water to make a single cotton T-shirt and 2,400 gallons (9,000 liters) to make a pair of jeans.

WHEN DOES FASHION GET FAST?

Fast fashion is the name given to the industry that turns the latest catwalk fashions into super-cheap items. For a few dollars, anyone can dress like a Hollywood celebrity, even though the clothes might not be well made or last very long. You might wear the outfit once and then throw it away.

Fast-fashion clothes are normally made of synthetic fibers, which are usually derived from plastic. This means we are using fossil fuels to make plastic clothes, which are very difficult to dispose of.

Seems a bit silly, doesn't it? Why would we waste our money and the planet's resources like that?

CLOTHES SHOCKER: In the US, 85 percent of textile waste is either burned or sent to a landfill.

OIL DRILLING

CHEMICAL PROCESS

MAKING

NYLON SWEATER

LANDFILL

SHOP

BUYING

SHIPPING

SHOPPING

PACKAGING

WHO MAKES OUR CLOTHES?

The problem isn't just about materials, transportation, or throwing old clothes away. A lot of fast fashion is produced in factories where people work in difficult conditions and are exposed to dangerous chemicals—with little pay and no rights.

WHAT CAN YOU DO ABOUT FASHION WASTE?

Everybody needs clothes, so you can't just stop buying and wearing them to save the planet! Clothes last only so long and will eventually fall apart, especially if you wear them often, wash them regularly, and rip them when you fall off your bike.

Lots of superheroes have their clothes bought for them by their parents or caregivers, but this doesn't mean you can't get involved with what you buy. If you wear a school uniform, it will often have to come from a shop, but everything else is fair game for change! You just need to decide on your look.

You can try to choose ethical brands or, even better, make your own clothes. It's a real skill but can be fun, is very useful, and may save you a lot of money. Start by learning to knit a scarf or hat and go from there! You can also easily make reusable face masks to keep your family and friends safe from viruses.

> YOUR 2-MINUTE MISSION: **Make a reusable face mask. There are lots of tutorials online, and all you need is an old, clean cotton T-shirt and some pieces of elastic. It will take you more than two minutes, but it will be fun—and it will cut down on waste!**
> **50 POINTS**

PLANET FASHION

You don't have to buy fast fashion. And you don't have to follow the crowd. Planet Fashion is the new way to dress for the future of a brighter world. Who will you be?

THE SLOW-FASHION FRIEND: Finds quality clothes that are made from natural fibers. Their clothes aren't cheap, but they last a long time.

THE SECONDHAND SUPERSTAR: Buys big brands secondhand from consignment stores or websites. Saves loads of money on their clothes.

THE THRIFT SHOP TRENDSETTER: Saves old clothes from going to waste. Their style is mix-and-match, cheap yet stylish!

THE DIY HERO: Has fun recycling old stuff and making it new by sewing, knitting, and just being creative.

REVAMP YOUR WARDROBE

You can also adapt what you own. Sort your clothes into piles: the ones that don't fit, the ones you never wear, clothes that need fixing or are worn out, and the clothes that you love and wear all the time.

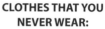

CLOTHES THAT DON'T FIT:
Give them to a thrift shop or a younger friend or a family member.

CLOTHES THAT YOU NEVER WEAR:
Customize them with badges, ribbons, or patches so you want to wear them. Or give them to a thrift store or sell them online with the help of your parents or caregivers.

CLOTHES THAT ARE WORN OUT:
Learn to sew and fix them up. Make them good as new and pass them on to someone else to enjoy.

CLOTHES THAT YOU LOVE:
Keep them. Love them. Wear them. When they get old, mend them!

YOUR 2-MINUTE MISSION: Revamp your wardrobe using one of the ideas above.
5 POINTS

EVERYDAY SUPERHERO

Name: Maggie

Job: Student

Superpower: Spotting a bargain

How you fight climate change: I buy secondhand clothes online or from thrift stores

Top tip: Buying secondhand saves money and the planet

Hates: Fast fashion

Loves: Finding a hidden gem

MAGGIE

FIGHT CLIMATE CHANGE WITH YOUR LAUNDRY

You already know why you need to save water when you wash your clothes. But don't forget that how you dry your clothes matters too. Once you've done your washing on a low heat, don't forget to say NO to the tumble dryer. Tumble-drying uses up loads of electricity. I know laundry isn't the most fun thing, but if you get involved and hang it out instead, you will not only help the planet but also get HIGH PRAISE from your family.

YOUR 2-MINUTE MISSION: **Become a clothespin champion. Next time you see the washing machine being unloaded, ask your parents or caregivers if you can hang your clothes to dry rather than use the dryer. 10 POINTS**

FIGHT CLIMATE CHANGE IN YOUR GARDEN

Your yard, garden, windowsill, balcony, local park, or school playground is a fantastic place to fight climate change. If we look after nature, we are looking after our ecosystems and helping the planet stay balanced. Any outside space, however small or unloved, has huge potential to be filled with flowers, insects, amphibians, mammals, and birds, no matter where you live. It's time to grab your superhero gardening gloves and get planting.

HOW YOUR GARDEN CAN HELP FIGHT CLIMATE CHANGE

As humans, we sometimes forget that nature is our friend on planet Earth. Instead we treat it as our enemy! We pull up weeds, cut down trees, and dig up grass to make way for concrete. But the more we look after plants and animals, the healthier our planet will be. You can make a difference by trying some small changes that will mean nature can thrive in your outside spaces.

A HELPING HAND FOR WILDLIFE

Nature is incredible, but sometimes it needs your help! Many mammals, birds, and insects that were once common in our backyards are facing tough times because the places they used to call home are no longer as welcoming. But the good news is there is lots you can do to provide shelter, food, and water for the birds, bugs, and frogs!

Feed the birds with a birdfeeder.

Add a birdbath or shallow bowl of water.

Make a log pile for creepy-crawlies.

Plant bee- and insect-friendly flowers.

Ban chemicals and pesticides.

YOUR 2-MINUTE MISSION: Make nature feel welcome in your green space by doing one—or all—of the above.
10 POINTS EACH

BELIEVE IN THE BEES

Bees are tiny but incredibly important. Their job is to pollinate plants. That means they carry pollen from the male parts of a flower to the female parts of another flower so the plant produce seeds and more plants grow. The sad fact is, bees are under threat because of habitat loss and climate change. Without bees and other pollinating insects, plants won't be able to reproduce. This could mean shortages in the crops we rely on for our food! You ca help by making a garden bee hotel, which will attract pollinating solitary bees looking for a safe place to make their nests.

YOUR 2-MINUTE MISSION: Make a bee hotel. 30 POINTS

YOU WILL NEED:
A small terra-cotta plant pot; hollow bamboo canes of different widths; modeling clay; string.

1. Ask an adult to cut the bamboo canes to a length that fits the depth of your pot.
2. Tie the bundle of canes together with a piece of string.
3. Place some modeling clay in the bottom of the pot and stick the bundle of canes into the clay.
4. Place your bee hotel somewhere it won't get wet, in a position where it has full sun with no vegetation in the way. In winter, bring it into a dry but cold place, like a garage. The bees will be safe and warm until spring!

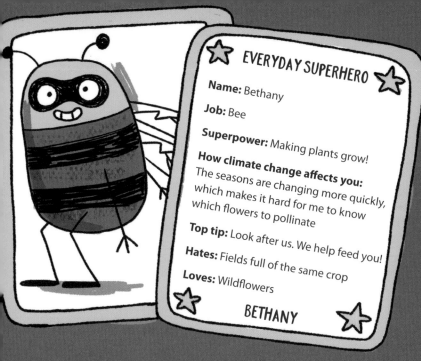

EVERYDAY SUPERHERO

Name: Bethany

Job: Bee

Superpower: Making plants grow!

How climate change affects you:
The seasons are changing more quickly, which makes it hard for me to know which flowers to pollinate

Top tip: Look after us. We help feed you!

Hates: Fields full of the same crop

Loves: Wildflowers

BETHANY

USE YOUR LAWN TO FIGHT CLIMATE CHANGE

Grass has the power to fight climate change. As it grows, it captures carbon dioxide. A really important part of our job fighting climate change is to help nature store carbon wherever it can—and that starts with your lawn. The best thing you can do is to let it grow wild. Lawns with longer grass will also make better homes for insects, birds, and other animals.

YOUR 2-MINUTE MISSION: **Talk to your parents or caregivers about letting your lawn grow a little longer. If your family likes a neat lawn, ask them to leave a section you can turn into a wildlife garden. When it grows, look out for flowers, bees, and insects.**
20 POINTS

HARVESTING RAINWATER

The supply of water contributes to climate change because of cleaning and pumping. But just imagine if there was a free source of water that you could collect and use to water your plants at any time! Oh, hang on! There is! Every time it rains, gallons of water pour down from the skies on your roof that can be used to water the garden instead of a hose!

**YOUR 2-MINUTE MISSION: Any big, watertight container will be suitable for catching rain as it comes off the roof of your home or school. With an adult's help, make sure your drainpipe can flow into the container. Ensure the container is open at the top and big enough to get a watering can into. Make sure that any overflow water can run off once it's full.
20 POINTS**

SUPER SOIL

Getting muddy isn't a problem for a planet-loving superhero! Healthy soil is important because it contains everything that's needed to grow plants and food. Without it, we'd be truly lost. Unhealthy soil, on the other hand, needs chemicals, pesticides, and fertilizers to grow plants.

One of the best ways to improve soil without chemicals is to add compost. And you can make your own. If you have space, a compost heap is great, as it gets rid of your vegetable peelings and garden waste. It also saves on the energy used to take the waste away. If you don't have space for one at home, your fruit, vegetable, and garden waste can often be collected by the town or city and turned into compost.

> **YOUR 2-MINUTE MISSION: You can make compost at home or at school to get rid of uncooked food waste, plant matter, and grass cuttings. Some paper and cardboard can also go in the compost. This mission will take more than two minutes, but it is very satisfying! 50 POINTS**

HOW TO MAKE COMPOST

1. Ask your parents or caregivers to help get you a compost bin. Some towns have community composting and may even be able to give you a bin!
2. Put the bin somewhere that doesn't get too hot or cold. It can go on the earth or on a hard surface.
3. Put some soil in it to start things off (a couple of spades from a flower bed).
4. Put your vegetable peelings, fruit scraps, and grass cuttings in it. Put the lid on.
5. Every so often, turn the compost with a garden fork to get air into it.
6. When it's broken down (in a few months), use it on your garden.

WHY WORMS ARE SOIL SUPERHEROES

- They eat parasites and break up roots.
- They get air into the soil.
- They aid drainage, allowing water to pass through soil.
  - They poop out worm casts, which are full of nutrients.

EVERYDAY SUPERHERO

Name: Wilf

Job: Worm

Superpower: Making soil healthy!

How climate change affects you: I have to balance greenhouse gases stored in the soil

Top tip: Even a tiny worm can change the world

Hates: Birds

Loves: Making casts

WILF

CITY GARDENING: GO UNDERCOVER

If you don't have a garden at home or live in a city where there isn't much outside space, you can still make room for wildlife and plants. Flowers and insects can thrive almost anywhere, so outdoor areas such as a windowsill or balcony or forgotten flower bed can be used to help nature. All you have to do is love it and look after it.

Look for places that need your superhero care. It could be a planter, a little flower bed no bigger than a pocket handkerchief, or a park that's been forgotten. Enlist the help of your older friends, family, and neighbors.

- Clear up any litter.
- Get help turning over the soil with a spade and clearing enough space around any existing plants for your seeds.
- Sow wildflower seeds in spring or autumn.
- Stand back, keep watering, and watch your seeds grow.

YOUR 2-MINUTE MISSION: **Be a guerrilla gardener by starting your own urban garden. Add a bee hotel and fallen sticks or logs to create homes for insects. What wildlife visits your garden?**
30 POINTS

FIGHT CLIMATE CHANGE WHEN YOU TRAVEL

How do you travel to school, to stores, or to see your friends and family? Do you go by car, bus, train, or bike? Or do you have a solar-powered flying carpet? Didn't think so!

The way you travel has a massive effect on climate change. Your mission as a #2minutesuperhero is to fight climate change by thinking about how you and your family travel day to day. Try to make changes wherever you can to reduce your impact on the planet. Every journey makes a difference.

WHAT'S THE MOST PLANET-FRIENDLY WAY TO TRAVEL?

As a **#2minutesuperhero**, to do your good work to save the planet, you are probably going to have to travel around a bit. But what's the best way to do it? Should you walk, ride your bike, get a lift, or take the bus? Let's roll—with a quiz!

YOUR 2-MINUTE MISSION: **It's time for the travel quiz! Put these modes of transportation in order, starting with the most planet-friendly method and finishing with the least.**
10 POINTS

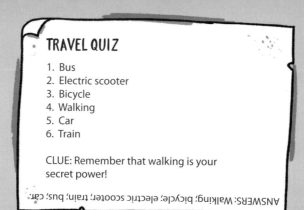

THE POWER BEHIND YOUR JOURNEY

Our transportation network is powered in lots of different ways. Fossil fuels are the most polluting and damaging for the planet, whereas electricity (especially if it comes from a renewable source) is much cleaner. But using your own power and traveling by bike or walking is the best of all!

CAR: Cars are powered by fossil fuels (gasoline or diesel), although electric cars are becoming more popular. Trips where only one person is traveling in the car are the least planet friendly.

BUS: Buses are normally powered by fossil fuels (gasoline or diesel), although hybrid (fossil fuels and electricity) and electric models exist. They can transport lots of people at once.

TRAIN: Trains are usually powered by electricity, although some use diesel. They can transport lots and lots of people at one time.

SCOOTER: Scooters are powered by a battery, which needs to be recharged using electricity.

BIKE AND FOOT: These are the greenest ways to travel—plus, using them is good for you.

CHANGE THE WAY YOU TRAVEL

It's time to think about the ways you travel. Next time you go anywhere, consider how planet friendly the trip is and whether you can cut out using the car and travel under your own steam. Can you choose a different way to get to school or your next baseball game or to see your family on the weekend?

HOW DO YOU TRAVEL NOW?	SAVE-THE-PLANET TRAVEL
CAR	~~CAR~~
WALK	WALK
~~SCOOTER~~	SCOOTER
~~BICYCLE~~	BICYCLE
~~BUS~~	BUS
~~TRAIN~~	TRAIN

YOUR 2-MINUTE MISSION: **Think about the trips you are going to make in the next week. Can you do one of these by public transportation, walking, or cycling? 10 POINTS FOR EACH TRIP**

WHY WALKING IS AMAZING

Have you ever thought that you could help the planet just by walking?

You can chat with friends and family while you walk.

You create zero carbon emissions (unless you fart!).

ALL ABOARD THE WALKING BUS

A walking bus is an organized walk to school for kids who are escorted by parents or caregivers. It's a great way to arrive each day. It is fun and healthy, and it can save your adults time spent dropping you off.

Walking is great for your entire family too!

Walking helps your health and fitness.

You get to really look at the world around you.

Walking helps improve your mental health and well-being.

YOUR 2-MINUTE MISSION: Is it possible for you to walk to school? If you don't walk but could, ask your school, parents, or caregivers to help organize a walking bus with kids who live nearby. **30 POINTS**

Within the image (card):

☆ **EVERYDAY SUPERHERO** ☆

Name: Pam

Job: Crossing guard

Superpower: I make it possible for kids to walk to school

How you fight climate change: I've helped kids cross the road for forty years

Top tip: Stop when you see my sign

Hates: Road rage

Loves: When kids say hello!

PAM

GETTING A LIFT TO SCHOOL

You might get driven to school because it's too far to walk, or because your parents or caregivers don't have time to walk with you. However, the ride to school is a big problem when it comes to greenhouse gases. The problem is even worse when you think that the trips are often short and it might only be you and the driver in the car, making it an inefficient use of energy.

SCHOOL RIDE NUMBERS: In the US each year, nearly 1 billion car trips are made to drop off or pick up kids from school!

If you can't travel to school any other way, a great option is to see if you can share a lift with someone who lives nearby. Get their parents or caregivers to talk to yours. If you can't find anyone, make a poster and put it up at school. Make a schedule for the morning and afternoon school rides. It will save time and money!

YOUR 2-MINUTE MISSION: **Start your own car pool and share the school ride with someone who lives near you. You might make a new friend as a bonus!**
30 POINTS

IT'S TIME TO GET ON YOUR BIKE!

Do you own a bicycle? Do your parents or caregivers own bicycles? Then use them! Cycling is one of the cleanest and greenest forms of transportation, as well as being healthy, cheap, and fun. You get to be out in the fresh air with lots of space around you too!

DO YOU PRACTICE BIKE SAFETY?

Some schools may offer bike safety lessons. These are lessons with professional instructors who will show you how to ride a bike safely. You'll ride between cones, learn how to signal, find out all about your bike, and get to be a superhero cyclist (no capes allowed, though).

YOUR 2-MINUTE MISSION: **Does your school offer bike safety lessons? If it does, sign up for them. If it doesn't, ask your teacher whether the school can offer them. 20 POINTS**

RIDE FOR FUN WITH YOUR FAMILY AND FRIENDS

Cycling is great fun to do with your family and friends too. There are miles and miles of traffic-free bike paths around the US that you can take where it's safe, clean, and easy to ride. Just remember your helmet and some delicious homemade snacks!

YOUR 2-MINUTE MISSION: **Plan a cycling day out! Find bike trail routes near you at www.traillink.com. 20 POINTS**

PEDAL POWER

If you can't bike to school or near where you live, then you need to do something about it. It's time to activate the activist in you! Write to your member of Congress or city council asking for safe, traffic-free cycling for all. Remind them that as well as being good for our health, bicycling is also good for the planet. YAY! Go for it, you two-wheeled cycling superhero! Now we're really traveling!

YOUR 2-MINUTE MISSION: **Write to your member of Congress or city council and ask for safe cycle routes in your local area so you can get to school, visit friends and family, and go to the store on two wheels.**
30 POINTS

FIGHT CLIMATE CHANGE ON YOUR VACATION

Everyone loves to go on vacation. I certainly do. The only trouble is . . . guess what?

Yes. Going on vacations—especially to places far away— increases your carbon footprint. But this doesn't mean you can't go anywhere. Of course not! Every #2minutesuperhero needs a break from their good deeds once in a while. But how you go on vacation matters, especially if you go away a few times a year and fly each time you do. It's time for a vacation shake-up!

WHAT'S THE GREENEST FORM OF TRANSPORTATION?

Put simply, per mile per passenger, air travel is the most polluting form of transportation, with train and bus travel being better. And, as you already know, walking and cycling, naturally, are way above those.

You may not be the one who decides where and how you go on vacation, but you can fight climate change by helping influence your family's decisions. The more days out and trips you can take as a family without traveling by plane, the more you will be helping the planet. And if you can cut out the car as much as possible and travel by train, bus, bike, or foot instead, even better!

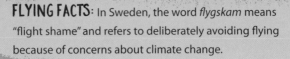

HOW TO HAVE A PLANET-FRIENDLY VACATION

You don't have to travel far to have a vacation or a day out to remember. In 2020, during the coronavirus pandemic, we learned how good it can be to stay in our own countries instead of flying thousands of miles for a bit of sun. Here are some more planet-friendly ideas:

- ♣ **A staycation:** Stay at home and relax, doing all your favorite things that you might not normally have time to do.
- ♣ **A local trip:** Go somewhere in your own state.
- ♣ **An adventure vacation:** Once you've reached your destination, don't use the car but instead do lots of fun outdoor things.
- ♣ **A cycling trip:** Travel by bike.
- ♣ **A hiking day:** Take a train and go walking.
- ♣ **A camping trip:** Choose an amazing campsite.

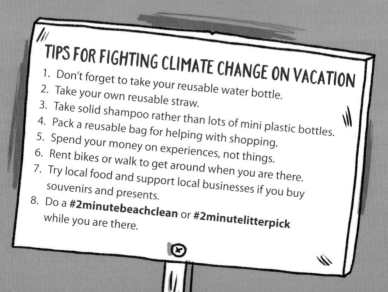

TIPS FOR FIGHTING CLIMATE CHANGE ON VACATION

1. Don't forget to take your reusable water bottle.
2. Take your own reusable straw.
3. Take solid shampoo rather than lots of mini plastic bottles.
4. Pack a reusable bag for helping with shopping.
5. Spend your money on experiences, not things.
6. Rent bikes or walk to get around when you are there.
7. Try local food and support local businesses if you buy souvenirs and presents.
8. Do a **#2minutebeachclean** or **#2minutelitterpick** while you are there.

WHY STAYCATIONS ARE FABULOUS!

Staycations are the best! They are vacations you take at home, where you can enjoy all the things you don't have time to do when you are at school or can't fit into a weekend. You don't have to travel, and they don't have to be expensive either!

Hang out with your friends.

Go for a long bike ride.

Go to a museum or art gallery.

Try a new sport or activity.

Find the best free thing to do near you.

Go for a long walk in the park or a nature reserve.

YOUR 2-MINUTE MISSION: Try one of these activities on your next staycation. **10 POINTS EACH**

Spend time with family.

Take the train to somewhere you've never been to before.

Take a day trip to the seaside, countryside, or city (depending on where you live!).

Save the planet!

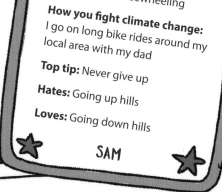

⭐ EVERYDAY SUPERHERO ⭐

Name: Sam

Job: Cyclist

Superpower: Freewheeling

How you fight climate change:
I go on long bike rides around my local area with my dad

Top tip: Never give up

Hates: Going up hills

Loves: Going down hills

SAM

FIGHT CLIMATE CHANGE AT THE SUPERMARKET

The supermarket is a great place to fight climate change because so much of what happens to our food—the way it's grown, transported, packaged, and then thrown away—can be bad for the planet. We're trying to cut down on our energy usage and help nature, right?

Some food is grown on land that used to be forest. Some food is grown on huge farms that support no other plants or wildlife, and some food is transported thousands of miles to reach our plates. We need to think about what we buy and where it comes from.

WHEN FOOD TAKES OVER THE FOREST

Growing food requires a lot of land—because there are a lot of us! In some places, like the rainforests in South America and Indonesia, trees get cut down to plant crops for either humans or animals to eat, or to create space to graze cattle. Our forests are vital to the health of the planet, as you know. Because trees absorb carbon dioxide, they are very important in the fight against climate change.

GOODBYE, FOREST: In 2017, data revealed that the world lost more than one soccer field of forest every second.

FOOD MILES

Supermarkets make it possible for us to have strawberries in the winter or a banana in our lunch box every day. We can have anything we want at almost any time of the year. But the problem is that transporting food thousands of miles via trucks, planes, and ships to our supermarket shelves creates greenhouse gases. We want to cut down on our food miles!

PACKAGING WASTE

How much of your household garbage is food packaging? A lot, I'll bet. Dealing with packaging is a big problem. It contributes to climate change because it takes energy to transport and recycle it. It also takes resources (oil and trees for plastic and paper, for example) to make it in the first place.

THINK LOCAL, SEASONAL, AND PLASTIC-FREE!

Before we were able to get food from anywhere in the world, we had to eat what grew close to where we lived. This meant our diet changed throughout the year as different foods grew in different seasons: strawberries in summer, apples in autumn, and brussels sprouts in winter! This is a better way to eat for the planet, as local food doesn't have to travel thousands of miles to get to us. If you can shop at farmers' markets or local shops, or have a produce box delivered, you will be doing excellent things—in terms of reducing both food miles and plastic waste!

YOUR 2-MINUTE MISSION: Next time you are in the produce section of the supermarket, look at the country where each item originated. Can you switch to something that has been grown closer to home or comes in plastic-free packaging?
10 POINTS

HIDDEN INGREDIENTS

Processed or packaged food—such as cookies, cereals, and sausages—are made with all kinds of ingredients. The trouble is that a lot of those ingredients are grown abroad, which means they have to be transported to the factories that make the food. Some ingredients are also grown on farms where trees have been cut down to grow the crops.

⭐ EVERYDAY SUPERHERO ⭐

Name: Archie

Job: Orangutan

Superpower: Being brave

How climate change affects you:
A digger cleared my forest to make space for palm oil

Top tip: Stop buying palm oil!

Hates: Being critically endangered

Loves: Being left alone in my forest

ARCHIE

DITCH THE PALM OIL

Palm oil is an ingredient that is used in all kinds of products, ranging from chips to noodles, from cookies to pizza, and from soap to face cream. It's cheap and useful and is an important crop for countries like Malaysia and Indonesia. The trouble is that there is such demand for it that rainforests are being cut down to grow it. This destroys habitats for animals such as orangutans and means the ecosystems across large areas of land are lost. The forest is gone forever. That's bad.

YOUR 2-MINUTE MISSION: **This is a great game! The next time you are at the supermarket with your parents or caregivers, look at the ingredients of each of the packaged foods or toiletries you buy. See if you can spot palm oil in the ingredients list. Look out for:**

vegetable oil, vegetable fat, palm kernel, palm kernel oil, palm fruit oil, sodium palmate, sodium palmitate, palm olein, glyceryl stearate, stearic acid, *Elaeis guineensis*, palmitic acid, palm stearin, palmitoyl oxostearamide, palmitoyl tetrapeptide-3, sodium laureth sulfate, sodium lauryl sulfate, sodium palm kernelate, sodium lauroyl lactylate, hydrogenated palm glycerides, ethyl palmitate, octyl palmitate, cetyl alcohol.

Can you choose an alternative with the RSPO logo, which certifies that any palm oil used in a product has been grown responsibly? If not, can you leave that item on the shelf? 20 POINTS

FIGHT CLIMATE CHANGE AT SCHOOL

On average, you spend around 180 days at school each year. That's a lot of your life! So why wouldn't you fight climate change at school as well as at home, in your garden, or on vacation? The answer is that you can and should and will!

If you think of your school as if it's your daytime home, then it's easy to come up with ways you can fight climate change, especially if you can get your teacher to join you on your #2minutesuperhero mission!

Some of the nicest, greenest, and most exciting people I know are teachers. And one thing I will bet you is that they want to save the world as much as you do. So what is your class waiting for?

ALL YOU HAVE TO DO IS TRY

Chances are that your teacher is already a secret superhero, working tirelessly behind the scenes. Teachers think up lesson plans and sports activities and do their best to make your time in the classroom great. That means they are busy. Very busy. So they might not have had time to think about how your class can fight climate change. But it's OK. You can talk to them about it and show that it is possible to make small but important changes in just two minutes.

SAVING ENERGY AT SCHOOL

Your school uses energy to turn the lights on, keep you warm, and power computers, printers, and all kinds of other stuff. And you know what that means: your school has a carbon footprint. The more you can help your school to reduce it, the more you can fight climate change!

TURN OFF ALL THE LIGHTS WHEN A CLASSROOM IS EMPTY OR SCHOOL IS FINISHED!
It'll save money too! Make labels for the light switches in your classroom to remind everyone to turn off the lights before they go home.

TURN OFF ALL THE COMPUTERS AT NIGHT! Make signs for each of the computers to remind everyone about it.

SAVE PAPER—AND TREES!
Write on both sides of a piece of paper and recycle when you're done!

SAVING WATER AT SCHOOL

Water is a precious resource, and it is important that we not waste it.

DON'T WASTE WATER!
When you wash your hands, turn the tap off as soon as you are done.

PUT ONLY PEE, POOP, PUKE, AND PAPER DOWN THE TOILET! Use the garbage can for bandages or trash, and avoid flushing the toilet unnecessarily.

REMEMBER YOUR REUSABLE WATER BOTTLE! If you have leftover water, use it to water plants in your classroom or school garden.

GOING GREEN

You've already learned about clean energy from solar power. Well, imagine if you could have all your classes powered by the Sun! Solar power can be used in your school to generate electricity and to heat water. It's awesome because as well as producing zero greenhouse gases, the Sun's power is without limit and free—and could even earn money back for your school. If your school doesn't yet have solar panels, now might be the time to talk to your teacher or principal about them. Even if installing solar panels doesn't happen immediately, you will have planted the seed of the idea!

YOUR 2-MINUTE MISSION: **Talk to your teacher about whether your school could use solar power. If the school hasn't considered it because it is too expensive to install, you could offer to organize a school fundraiser.**
50 POINTS

⭐ EVERYDAY SUPERHERO ⭐

Job: Your teacher

Superpower: Making learning fun

How you fight climate change: We help kids find ways to save the planet

Top tip: Believe in yourself!

Hates: Budget cuts

Loves: Hearing about how you are going to save the planet

TEACHER

REDUCING WASTE AT SCHOOL

Waste removal is expensive. It's also bad for the planet. So reducing what goes in the trash is another great way to fight climate change. It will also save your school money!

WASTE FACT: The average school in the US wastes approximately 39 pounds (more than 17 kilograms) of food per student per year.

PAPER WASTE

A lot of waste created by schools is paper and comes from photocopying, printing, worksheets, and notebooks.

> **YOUR 2-MINUTE MISSION: If your school doesn't have one already, ask your teacher about setting up a recycling station for paper waste in your classroom.**
> **10 POINTS**

> **YOUR 2-MINUTE MISSION: Earn points for your school as a TerraCycle public drop-off location. Gather old pens, printer cartridges, and chip bags for recycling.**
> **Go to www.terracycle.com to find out more.**
> **30 POINTS**

FOOD WASTE

Food waste is a big problem for schools. All food has a carbon footprint, whether from growing, transporting, or cooking it. If you waste food, then it also has to be transported to a garbage or compost facility, where it may produce methane, a climate gas, as it breaks down.

I happen to know that all **#2minutesuperheroes** love lunch! But you might be in too much of a rush to eat all your food or you might not like the option that day or you might not be hungry when lunch comes around. All these things can add up to make a lot of food waste.

> **YOUR 2-MINUTE MISSION: You can help fight climate change just by eating all your lunch—including all your fruits and vegetables. If you can't eat them all, ask for smaller portions. Encourage your friends to do the same. 20 POINTS**

PLASTIC WASTE

Yogurt cups, plastic straws, candy wrappers, soda cans or bottles . . . There's a long list of single-use plastic items in your school bag or lunch box that might be thrown away when they could be recycled or, best of all, switched for reusable alternatives!

> **YOUR 2-MINUTE MISSION: Bring your packed lunch in reusable containers that you will use again and again. 10 POINTS**

> **YOUR 2-MINUTE MISSION: With the help of your teacher, set up recycling bins where you have your lunch. 20 POINTS**

FIGHT CLIMATE CHANGE BY PLANTING TREES

All life on Earth—including humans—depends on the relationships that exist between living things. Plants need animals to spread their seeds, insects need habitats to live, birds need grasses for food, and we also need food to survive. The problems occur when these relationships break down.

Hopefully, you've now got lots of great ideas for looking after insects, birds, and other animals in your gardens or outside spaces, but what about plants and trees? When it comes to the fight against climate change, these are some of the greatest superheroes of all.

WHY TREES AND PLANTS ARE SUPER IMPORTANT

Just like you, trees and plants can make a massive difference to planet Earth.

Trees and plants (which include things such as seaweed and tiny plants called phytoplankton in the oceans) produce food through a process called photosynthesis. Plants use sunlight, water, and carbon dioxide to produce energy that fuels new growth (leaves, branches, and flowers). As part of this process, plants give off oxygen and moisture, which we then use to breathe. Amazing!

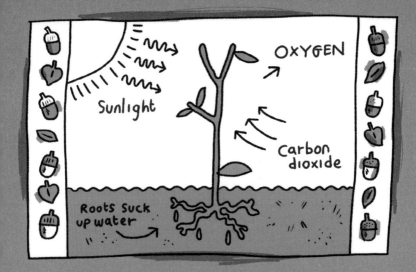

Sunlight

OXYGEN

Carbon dioxide

Roots suck up water

If there aren't enough trees or plants to absorb all the carbon dioxide we are producing, then the level of carbon dioxide will continue to rise. And that will make the greenhouse effect even worse. So what can you do? Plant a tree, of course!

YOUR 2-MINUTE MISSION: **Although it is simple to plant a tree from a seed, it will take longer than two minutes for it to grow into a tree! But some trees can live to be thousands of years old, so your two minutes can have a long-lasting effect. 50 POINTS**

1. Collect seeds, such as acorns, from trees in the autumn.
2. Find a pot with drainage holes and put a stone at the bottom and then fill the pot with compost.
3. Put two seeds in the pot about 1 inch (2 centimeters) deep and water them.
4. Put the pot outside in a shady corner. You can cover the pot with mesh to stop animals from digging up the seeds.
5. Keep the seeds watered. As they grow, transfer them to bigger pots.
6. When they are 15 inches (40 centimeters) tall, plant them in the ground so they can grow big and tall.

FIGHT CLIMATE CHANGE WITH YOUR MONEY

Empty your pockets or backpack! What's in there? Have you got any coins stashed away among the fluff? I bet you have. Your money is a powerful thing. Believe it or not, how you spend those coins can have an effect on climate change. Your money can change the world! Imagine that!

CHOOSE WHAT YOU BUY CAREFULLY

How do you spend your money? Do you buy candy, toys, books, or games? Or do you save up for days out or gear for your bike? Here are some top ideas for how to spend your dough AND love the planet.

DO	DON'T
✓ Avoid things in unnecessary packaging.	✗ Fall for fancy packaging. It's all waste and doesn't help climate change.
✓ Spend it on books or experiences, like going to the movies or a local attraction.	✗ Buy things you will play with only once before putting them in a drawer or throwing them away.
✓ Buy things secondhand from garage sales or thrift stores.	✗ Buy new things if you can get them secondhand.
✓ Save up for something you will use for many years, like a bike.	✗ Keep upgrading to the latest gadget.

YOUR 2-MINUTE MISSION: The next time you have some money saved up, think before you spend! Can you make one planet-friendly switch?
15 POINTS

JOIN A WILDLIFE GROUP

Lots of wildlife conservation charities have clubs that you can join. Your money will then help them to continue saving orangutans, polar bears, and lots of other endangered animals. In return, they send out magazines and activity packs that will give you ideas for how you can fight climate change, habitat destruction, and species extinction. Double win!

SPONSOR AN ANIMAL

Lots of animals in wildlife parks, nature reserves, and animal refuges—especially endangered species—can be sponsored. In exchange, you can get a certificate and an information pack about your animal. Imagine knowing that your allowance or birthday present is helping an animal that needs protection. How cool would it be to have a seal pup, polar bear, otter, or eagle of your own? Exciting!

FIGHT CLIMATE CHANGE WITH YOUR VOICE

Are you ready for the most important mission of all? This is the one where you use your voice to fight climate change. It's the bit where you get to shout. This mission is all about learning to stand up for what you believe in. It's not always easy being a climate activist—and that's what you need to become to complete the mission—but I know you can do it!

WHY THE PLANET NEEDS YOUR VOICE

The planet needs someone to stand up for it. Someone who can be brave and fierce enough to tell companies and governments to do more to protect the planet.

Nature needs you too. Because turtles, rhinos, and leopards can't talk! But you can.

HOW TO BE AN ACTIVIST

Using your voice to fight climate change means letting people know that you are not happy about the way things are. It means saying what you think and making sure that the people who are in power hear you and then, hopefully, make changes.

One of the first things to decide is exactly what you are asking for when you use your voice—whether that's at school or on a march. If people don't know why you are campaigning, they won't be able to do anything. So make sure you know! What is it you want?

More recycling? More bicycle lanes? More trees? More renewable energy? More pandas? You decide!

HOW TO BE AN AMAZING ACTIVIST

Be prepared!

Know what you want to say and be willing to listen to others.

Make yourself heard, but don't damage property or do anything that could get you in trouble.

Give thoughtful, respectful responses to people who don't understand why you are being an activist.

Don't be put off by people being rude. You have the support of millions.

YOU CAN BE AN ACTIVIST!

WHAT CHANGES DO YOU WANT TO SEE AT YOUR SCHOOL?

Think about what you would like to see happen at your school. What can you do to help? Start a collection point for plastic recycling? Organize a playground litter pick? Start a school garden? Hold a climate change assembly? There are so many things you can campaign for that will make a difference.

YOUR 2-MINUTE MISSION: **Choose what you want to campaign for. Get the support of your parents or caregivers, class, and teacher by talking to them politely about the issue. You could start a petition with signatures to show how many people agree with the change you are proposing. 30 POINTS**

JOIN A SCHOOL PROTEST

Greta Thunberg started protesting about climate change in August 2018 when she was fifteen. To start with, the protests involved standing outside the Swedish parliament building every Friday when she would ordinarily have been at school. She called it the School Strike for Climate. She has since become an acclaimed activist and has traveled all around the world to talk about the action we need to take. Greta and other young activists, such as Xiye Bastida from Mexico and Leah Namugerwa from Uganda, are agents of change who have influenced millions.

You can join school strikes too, although striking without permission from your parents or caregivers and the school can get you in trouble. Make sure you have a conversation with both before you do anything.

JOIN A PROTEST OR MARCH

Protests or marches are another great way to show that you—and hundreds or thousands of others—care about an issue. It's easy to make a sign or placard to take with you on protests. Your placard could be just a few words, a picture, or a list of demands. It's up to you!

YOUR 2-MINUTE MISSION:
With your family or caregivers, go on a march or protest against climate change.
30 POINTS

YOUR 2-MINUTE MISSION:
Make your own placard.
20 POINTS

THERE IS NO PLANET B!

FIGHT CLIMATE CHANGE WITH YOUR PEN

Congratulations on becoming an incredible, brilliant, planet-saving #2minutesuperhero! By completing all the missions in this book, you've done a huge amount to fight climate change and make a difference. I want to leave you with one final bonus mission, if you really want to get your voice heard.

WRITE A LETTER TO YOUR LOCAL GOVERNMENT

Writing letters to your member of Congress, senator, or city council lets them know about the issues you are worried about. If it's climate change, it is important that they hear from you. They have a duty to read your letter and should reply to you. They also have to listen to your concerns.

> **YOUR 2-MINUTE MISSION:** Write a letter to your member of Congress or city council. What do you think they could do better? Tell them what matters to you and what you want to change.
> **100 POINTS**

ear [insert name of congressperson or city councilor here],

My name is [INSERT YOUR NAME HERE]. I am [YOUR AGE HERE] and I attend [YOUR SCHOOL NAME HERE]. I am writing to you because I am worried about climate change. I already do lots to make a difference at home and school, but I'm worried it's not enough.

I have reduced my carbon footprint by walking to school whenever I can, but I can't make the rules that make it easier for people to buy electric cars, invest in renewable energy, and travel by train more cheaply than flying. You can.

I might be able to turn off the faucet when I brush my teeth and avoid wasting food, but I can't call the bosses of industry and tell them to stop destroying the planet for the sake of profit. You can.

And while I can encourage my fellow students to recycle more, create less waste, and remember to turn the lights off at home, I can't pass laws that make companies turn off their office lights at night and do all they can to save electricity. You can.

So I wanted to ask you: Are you doing all these things? And if not, why not?

The climate emergency is the most important issue of our time and will define the rest of my life. The climate is changing, and I believe we should all be doing EVERYTHING we can to make changes now, not in two, five, or twenty years' time.

I look forward to your reply.
Yours,
[SIGN HERE]

MISSION COMPLETED

Dear newly qualified #2minutesuperhero,

Climate change isn't an easy thing to fight, is it? It's not like fighting aliens or chasing after a runaway trampoline in a storm. It's more like trying to fight an idea that keeps changing its shape every time you think you've got it. You can't see it or touch it, and yet it could affect us all.

If you've read this book and completed some of the missions, you are making a big difference.

You might not be able to see it yet, but it all counts.

You've already proved that you can change if you have to because of the pandemic. Now that you've read this book, you've made some more amazing changes to your life that I hope you'll enjoy for years to come.

You've walked to school, saved electricity and resources, cooked delicious food, planted a tree, welcomed nature into your life, made a home for bees, learned to love the worms, cut out palm oil, made your voice heard, drawn a placard, spent a day eating meat-free, and written to your local government. WOW!

You may also have spoken about climate change with your classmates and teachers and started to make changes in your school. As a result, your school could be saving hundreds of gallons of water, spending less on electricity, and producing less waste at lunchtime! You, the **#2minutesuperhero**, are INCREDIBLE!

Think about what your actions mean. Imagine you've just thrown a pebble into a huge, calm pond. The pebble sinks with a splash that sends out ripples across the pond in all directions. Somewhere far away, in a place you may never see or hear about, the ripples reach chameleons whose chances of survival have changed because they now have enough to eat in their part of the forest. Somewhere else, on an icy hillside, far to the north, another ripple reaches an Arctic fox who has been able to raise her cubs because there's enough snow for them to remain hidden. They survive in their ecosystems because of you. You, your family, and friends helped to do that.

So, from me, and all the other everyday superheroes, thank you for all you do.

But don't stop! Because the fight for our planet is only just beginning.

With love and luck,
Martin

YOUR SUPERHERO RATING . . .

SUPERHERO POINTS

Now that you've finished your training, it's time to find out what kind of superhero you are. Add up the points you've earned by completing your missions.

MISSION 1: COUNT YOUR CARBON

Next time it's sunny, find a greenhouse or a room with a big window. When the light shines through the glass, what happens to the temperature inside? If you can find a thermometer, measure the temperature outside and inside and calculate the difference. **5 POINTS**

Think about your carbon footprint. Can you come up with one small action you could take tomorrow to reduce it? **10 POINTS**

TOTAL MISSION POINTS: 15

MISSION 2: YOU'VE GOT THE POWER

THINK ENERGY! Think about what you've done today. Did it use energy? What kinds of energy did it use? **10 POINTS**

Where does your energy come from? Some companies offer electricity from renewable sources. Talk to your parents or caregivers about it. **30 POINTS**

TOTAL MISSION POINTS: 40

MISSION 3: FIGHT CLIMATE CHANGE AT HOME

Count up the rooms in your house where there are devices that are regularly left on standby. Make a sign for each one that says: NOT IN USE? CUT THE JUICE! **20 POINTS**

Make a chart with the name of each family member on it. Every time someone turns off a light when they leave a room, give them a gold star. Who is the most energy-efficient? **10 POINTS**

Close doors when you leave a room—this will stop heat from escaping. **5 POINTS**

Close curtains at night to keep heat in. **5 POINTS**

Put on a sweater—not the heat—if you feel a bit chilly. **5 POINTS**

Use an extra blanket on your bed instead of turning up the heat. **5 POINTS**

Get some woolly socks or superhero slippers to put on when you come home from school so you don't get cold feet. **5 POINTS**

Does your heating go on and off at set times? Ask your parents or caregivers if you can change the settings slightly. An hour less a day will make a difference! **10 POINTS**

Watch your favorite programs together instead of separately, as if you were at the movies, with popcorn and goodies. It'll be fun, and it will help save the planet too! **10 POINTS**

Put yourself in charge of the recycling in your house. You are king or queen of collection day. Make sure all your recycling is ready to go into the right bin. **10 POINTS**

TOTAL MISSION POINTS: 85

MISSION 4: FIGHT CLIMATE CHANGE WITH YOUR FOOD

If you're a meat lover, ask your family if you can go one day without eating any meat at all. It's a simple thing, but it will make a difference, especially if you make it a weekly thing. **20 POINTS**

Check the database of the Monterey Bay Aquarium Seafood Watch (www.seafoodwatch.org) to see if the fish you eat regularly is environmentally sustainable. Can you either cut it out or switch to a more ocean-friendly option if it scores poorly? **20 POINTS**

Next time you have the option to choose veggies over meat (your packed-lunch sandwich filling, your school-lunch choice, your after-school snack), say yes to plant power! **20 POINTS**

Try a milk alternative on your breakfast cereal. Think about where the alternative is grown and how it is packaged. Can it be recycled? **10 POINTS**

If you can't finish your dinner, rather than toss it, pop it in a container and save it for a snack or dinner the next day. Cold pizza is great, and curries and chili are always better on day two. FACT! **5 POINTS**

TOTAL MISSION POINTS: 75

MISSION 5: FIGHT CLIMATE CHANGE WITH YOUR SINK, SHOWER, AND TOILET

Make a water-saving device for your toilet tank with your parents or caregivers. **20 POINTS**

Do one of these water-saving activities each day. **5 POINTS EACH X 5**

TOTAL MISSION POINTS: 45

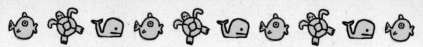

MISSION 6: FIGHT CLIMATE CHANGE WITH YOUR (LACK OF) STUFF

Spread all your toys over your bedroom floor. Pick out the ones you have used in the last few months. Put them in one pile. Put the rest, including stuff that's broken or missing parts, in another pile. **5 POINTS**

Donate your toys to a charity shop and help raise money for a good cause. **10 POINTS**

Donate your toys to a toy drive so other kids can play with them for free. **10 POINTS**

Give away your old toys to children who are younger than you who will love playing with them. **10 POINTS**

Hold a garage sale and sell toys you don't use. **10 POINTS**

Next time you get asked about what you would like for your birthday, think about the activities you love to do. Suggest an experience rather than more stuff. **20 POINTS**

TOTAL MISSION POINTS: 65

MISSION 7: FIGHT CLIMATE CHANGE WITH YOUR GADGETS

Ask a parent or caregiver if you can unplug a gadget that isn't used regularly but is left on standby. **5 POINTS**

Go through your old gadgets. If they don't work, see if they can be repaired. If they can't, then recycle them. If they work, give them away or ask a parent or caregiver to help you sell them. **20 POINTS**

TOTAL MISSION POINTS: 25

MISSION 8: FIGHT CLIMATE CHANGE WITH YOUR WARDROBE

Make a reusable face mask. There are lots of tutorials online, and all you need is an old, clean cotton T-shirt and some pieces of elastic. It will take you more than two minutes, but it will be fun—and it will cut down on waste! **50 POINTS**

Revamp your wardrobe using one of the ideas on page 72. **5 POINTS**

Become a clothespin champion. Next time you see the washing machine being unloaded, ask your parents or caregivers if you can hang your clothes to dry rather than use the dryer. **10 POINTS**

TOTAL MISSION POINTS: 65

MISSION 9: FIGHT CLIMATE CHANGE IN YOUR YARD

Make nature feel welcome in your green space by doing one—or all—of the tasks on page 75.
10 POINTS EACH X 5

Make a bee hotel. **30 POINTS**

Talk to your parents or caregivers about letting your lawn grow a little longer. If your family likes a neat lawn, ask them to leave a section you can turn into a wildlife garden. When it grows, look out for flowers, bees, and insects. **20 POINTS**

Any big, watertight container will be suitable for catching rain as it comes off the roof of your home or school. With an adult's help, make sure your drainpipe can flow into the container. Ensure the container is open at the top and big enough to get a watering can into. Make sure that any overflow water can run off once it's full. **20 POINTS**

You can make compost at home or at school to get rid of uncooked food waste, plant matter, and grass cuttings. Some paper and cardboard can also go in the compost. This mission will take more than two minutes, but it is very satisfying! **50 POINTS**

Be a guerrilla gardener by starting your own urban garden. Add a bee hotel and fallen sticks or logs to create homes for insects. What wildlife visits your garden?
30 POINTS

TOTAL MISSION POINTS: 200

MISSION 10: FIGHT CLIMATE CHANGE WHEN YOU TRAVEL

It's time for the travel quiz! Put these modes of transportation in order, starting with the most planet-friendly method and finishing with the least. **10 POINTS**

Think about the trips you are going to make in the next week. Can you do one of these by public transportation, walking, or cycling? **10 POINTS FOR EACH TRIP**

Is it possible for you to walk to school? If you don't walk but could, ask your school, parents, or caregivers to help organize a walking bus with kids who live nearby. **30 POINTS**

Start your own car pool and share the school ride with someone who lives near you. You might make a new friend as a bonus! **30 POINTS**

Does your school offer bike safety lessons? If it does, sign up for them!

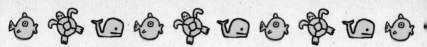

If it doesn't, ask your teacher if the school can offer them. **20 POINTS**

Plan a cycling day out! Find bike trail routes near you at www.traillink.com. **20 POINTS**

Write to your member of Congress or city council and ask for safe cycle routes in your local area so you can get to school, visit friends and family, and go to the store on two wheels. **30 POINTS**

TOTAL MISSION POINTS: 140 + your trip points

MISSION 11: FIGHT CLIMATE CHANGE ON YOUR VACATION

Try one of the activities on pages 92–93 on your next staycation. **10 POINTS EACH X 9**

TOTAL MISSION POINTS: 90

MISSION 12: FIGHT CLIMATE CHANGE AT THE SUPERMARKET

Next time you are in the produce section of the supermarket, look at the country where each item originated. Can you switch to something that has been grown closer to home or comes in plastic-free packaging? **10 POINTS**

This is a great game! The next time you are at the supermarket with your parents and caregivers, look at the ingredients of each of the packaged foods or toiletries you buy. See if you can spot palm oil in the ingredients list. Look out for: vegetable oil, vegetable fat, palm kernel, palm kernel oil, palm fruit oil, sodium palmate, sodium palmitate, palm olein, glyceryl stearate, stearic acid, *Elaeis guineensis*, palmitic acid, palm stearin, palmitoyl oxostearamide, palmitoyl tetrapeptide-3, sodium laureth sulfate, sodium lauryl sulfate, sodium palm kernelate, sodium lauroyl lactylate, hydrogenated palm glycerides, ethyl palmitate, octyl palmitate, cetyl alcohol. Can you choose an alternative with the RSPO logo, which certifies that any palm oil used in the product has been grown responsibly? If not, can you leave that item on the shelf? **20 POINTS**

TOTAL MISSION POINTS: 30

MISSION 13: FIGHT CLIMATE CHANGE AT SCHOOL

Talk to your teacher about whether your school could use solar power. If the school hasn't considered it because it is too expensive to install, you could offer to organize a school fundraiser. **50 POINTS**

If your school doesn't have one already, ask your teacher about setting up a recycling station for paper waste in your classroom. **10 POINTS**

Earn points for your school as a TerraCycle public drop-off location. Collect old pens, printer cartridges, and chip bags for recycling. Go to www.terraycle.com to find out more. **30 POINTS**

You can help fight climate change just by eating all your lunch—including all your fruits and vegetables. If you can't eat them all, ask for smaller portions. Encourage your friends to do the same. **20 POINTS**

Bring your packed lunch in reusable containers that you will use again and again. **10 POINTS**

With the help of your teacher, set up recycling bins where you have your lunch. **20 POINTS**

TOTAL MISSION POINTS: 140

MISSION 14: FIGHT CLIMATE CHANGE BY PLANTING TREES

Although it is simple to plant a tree from a seed, it will take longer than two minutes to grow into a tree! But some trees can live to be thousands of years old, so your two minutes can have a long-lasting effect. **50 POINTS**

TOTAL MISSION POINTS: 50

MISSION 15: FIGHT CLIMATE CHANGE WITH YOUR MONEY

The next time you have some money saved up, think before you spend! Can you make one planet-friendly switch? **15 POINTS**

TOTAL MISSION POINTS: 15

MISSION 16: FIGHT CLIMATE CHANGE WITH YOUR VOICE

Choose what you want to campaign for. Get the support of your parents or caregivers, class, and teacher by talking to them politely about the issue. You could start a petition with signatures to show how many people agree with the change you are proposing. **30 POINTS**

With your family or caregivers, go on a march or protest against climate change. **30 POINTS**

Make your own placard. **20 POINTS**

TOTAL MISSION POINTS: 80

BONUS MISSION: FIGHT CLIMATE CHANGE WITH YOUR PEN

Write a letter to your member of Congress or city council. What do you think they could do better? Tell them what matters to you and what you want to change. **100 POINTS**

TOTAL MISSION POINTS: 100

WHAT KIND OF SUPERHERO ARE YOU?

Now that you've completed the 2-minute missions, add up your points. What kind of #2minutesuperhero are you?

0–499 POINTS

Someone once told me that it's the doing that matters. And that's what makes you an awesome superhero. From a standing start, you've raced ahead of the pack. You're now doing stuff that might be a little boring or difficult or challenging, and you're doing it brilliantly. I salute you for it. We don't need you to be perfect. You just have to try, to care, and to get on with saving the world. You're doing it. Well done! Now it's time to get more of those missions accomplished so I can award you that four-star status.

MISSION COMPLETE: You're a 3 ★ Superhero!

500–999 POINTS

You, my superhero friend, have got the whole superhero thing going on. You are doing, and you are achieving. You've done a lot of great things for the planet, and I thank you for it. You've let nature into your life, planted a tree, and maybe even written to your congressperson. Did you get a reply yet? Don't worry if you didn't. We need more yous, not more them.

What's next for a superhero like you? Cash in your chips, or go for gold? If I were you, I'd carry on and go for five-star status! You can do it. GO, YOU!

MISSION COMPLETE: You are a proper 4 ★ Superhero!

OVER 1,000 POINTS

Goodness me! The planet needs more people like you. You've completed all your missions and have scored a whole load of points. What does that mean? The planet is a nicer place because of you. You've done your bit and improved the world. You can feel good knowing that those ripples are making a difference, wherever they go. Top marks. Thank you, and well done!

MISSION COMPLETE: You get the 5 ★ Superhero Award!

IMAGINE YOUR PHOTO HERE

EVERYDAY SUPERHERO

What's your name?

What's your job?

What's your superpower?

How do you fight climate change?

What's your top tip?

What do you hate?

What do you love?

YOU

FIND OUT MORE ABOUT THE FIGH AGAINST CLIMATE CHANGE

Want to find out more? Excellent! Take a look at these:

CAMPAIGNS AND ACTIVISM

Fridays for Future: A charity set up by kids for kids
www.fridaysforfuture.org

Global Climate Strike: The essentials—how to, where to, and why
www.globalclimatestrike.net

Extinction Rebellion: Look for family events and local family groups.
www.extinctionrebellion.us

The Eden Project: A charity that does more than just grow plants in the world's coolest biomes. They also have cool stuff online!
www.edenproject.com/learn/for-everyone

The World Wildlife Fund: Another charity with fabulous online resources for superheroes
www.worldwildlife.org/teaching-resources

RESOURCES

Free teachers' resources for this book are available at
www.beachclean.shop/product-category/books/

ABOUT THE AUTHOR

Hello. I am Martin Dorey. I'm a surfer, writer, beach lover, and anti-plastic and climate change activist. I live near the sea in Cornwall, England, with my partner, Lizzy, who is also known as Dr. Seaweed. She's a gardener and botanist and helps me to understand plants and photosynthesis and all that exciting stuff! My children, Maggie and Charlotte, live down the road from me with their dog, Bob. Maggie is a lifeguard, and Charlotte makes a lot of her own clothes. I like surfing, walking, being outside, and trying to grow vegetables. I also cook a lot, especially when I'm in my camper van. I also like my bike, cleaning beaches, and waking up to sunny days by the sea with the people I love the most.

ABOUT THE 2 MINUTE FOUNDATION

The 2 Minute Foundation (www.2minute.org) is a charity that is devoted to cleaning up the planet two minutes at a time. The idea is very simple: each time you go to the beach, the park, or anywhere at all, take two minutes to pick up litter, take a picture of it, and then post it to social media to inspire others to do the same.

In 2014, we set up a network of eight Beach Clean Stations around Cornwall, England, that make it really easy for people to pick up litter at the beach. Today, in 2021, we have more than eight hundred of them! We have thousands of followers who help the planet every day by cleaning beaches, cutting out plastic from their lives, or picking up litter from the streets where they live.

With thanks to:

Lizzy;

Tim Wesson;

Daisy, Laurissa, and all at Walker Books;

Nicky, Dolly, Jodie, Jaik, Claire, Heather, Alan, Tab, Adam, Melvyn,
Kate, Andy, Emma, and the awesome 2 Minute Team;

the **#2minutebeachclean** family;

Chris Hines;

my superheroes: Adam, Charlie, Sam;

Fjällräven, Surfdome, the Eden Project, Friends of the Earth,
Extinction Rebellion;

and anyone else who has made an effort, no matter how small,
to make a difference.